T0285922

FAITH
over
FEAR

FAITH

over

FEAR

*100 Devotions
to Rest in the Shadow
of His Wings*

A Guideposts Devotional

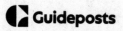 

ZONDERVAN BOOKS

Faith over Fear
Copyright © 2023 by Guideposts. All rights reserved.

Published in Grand Rapids, Michigan, by Zondervan. Zondervan is a registered trademark of The Zondervan Corporation, L.L.C., a wholly owned subsidiary of HarperCollins Christian Publishing, Inc.

Requests for information should be addressed to customercare@harpercollins.com.

Zondervan titles may be purchased in bulk for educational, business, fundraising, or sales promotional use. For information, please email SpecialMarkets@Zondervan.com.

ISBN 978-0-310-36689-8 (hardcover)
ISBN 978-0-310-36692-8 (audio)
ISBN 978-0-310-36690-4 (ebook)

Acknowledgments: Every attempt has been made to credit the sources of copyrighted material used in this book. If any such acknowledgment has been inadvertently omitted or miscredited, receipt of such information would be appreciated.

Scripture quotations marked (AMP) are taken from the Amplified Bible. Copyright © 2015 by The Lockman Foundation, La Habra, California. All rights reserved. • Scripture quotations marked (AMPC) are taken from the Amplified Bible, Classic Edition. Copyright © 2015 by The Lockman Foundation, La Habra, California. All rights reserved. • Scripture quotations marked (CEB) are taken from the Common English Bible. Copyright © 2011 by Common English Bible. • Scripture quotations marked (CSB) are taken from The Christian Standard Bible. Copyright © 2017 by Holman Bible Publishers. Used by permission. • Scripture quotations marked (ESV) are taken from the Holy Bible, English Standard Version. Copyright © 2001 by Crossway Bibles, a division of Good News Publishers. Used by permission. All rights reserved. • Scripture quotations marked (GNT) are taken from the Holy Bible, Good News Translation. Copyright © 1992 by American Bible Society. • Scripture quotations marked (ISV) are taken from the Holy Bible, International Standard Version. Copyright © 1995–2014 by ISV Foundation. All rights reserved internationally. Used by permission of Davidson Press, LLC. • Scripture quotations marked (JPS) are taken from Tanakh: A New Translation of the Holy Scriptures according to the Traditional Hebrew Text. Copyright © 1985 by the Jewish Publication Society. All rights reserved. • Scripture quotations marked (KJV) are taken from the King James Version of the Bible. • Scripture quotations marked (MSG) are taken from The Message. Copyright © 1993, 1994, 1995, 1996, 2000, 2001, 2002 by Eugene H. Peterson. • Scripture quotations marked (NASB and NASB1995) are taken from the New American Standard Bible®. Copyright © 1960, 1971, 1977, 1995, 2020 by The Lockman Foundation. All rights reserved. • Scripture quotations marked (NIV) are taken from The Holy Bible, New International Version. Copyright © 1973, 1978, 1984, 2011 by Biblica, Inc. Used by permission of Zondervan. All rights reserved worldwide. zondervan.com • Scripture quotations marked (NKJV) are taken from The Holy Bible, New King James Version. Copyright © 1982 by Thomas Nelson. • Scripture quotations marked (NLT) are taken from the Holy Bible, New Living Translation. Copyright © 1996, 2004, 2007 by Tyndale House Foundation. Used by permission of Tyndale House Publishers Inc., Carol Stream, Illinois. All rights reserved. • Scripture quotations marked (NRSV) are taken from the New Revised Standard Version Bible. Copyright © 1989 by the Division of Christian Education of the National Council of the Churches of Christ in the United States of America. Used by permission. All rights reserved. • Scripture quotations marked (RSV) are taken from the Revised Standard Version of the Bible. Copyright © 1946, 1952, 1971 by the Division of Christian Education of the National Council of the Churches of Christ in the United States of America. Used by permission. • Scripture quotations marked (TLB) are taken from The Living Bible. Copyright © 1971 by Tyndale House Publishers, Inc., Carol Stream, Illinois. All rights reserved.

Any internet addresses (websites, blogs, etc.) and telephone numbers in this book are offered as a resource. They are not intended in any way to be or imply an endorsement by Zondervan, nor does Zondervan vouch for the content of these sites and numbers for the life of this book.

Cover and interior design by Pam Walker, W Design Studio
Cover photo by Shutterstock
Typeset by Aptara, Inc.

Printed in the United States of America

23 24 25 26 27 LBC 5 4 3 2 1

*There are only two responses
to the world: fear or love. Your life
depends on which one you choose.*

—DEEPAK CHOPRA, AUTHOR

Contents

Introduction

Choosing Faith over Fear

CAROL KUYKENDALL

What is your earliest memory?" I was asked in a seminar on Life Memories.

I had to dig deep to find an answer, but slowly a scene came to mind.

I was three or four years old in our church Sunday school room with a couple other children. We were the last left, waiting for our parents to come get us. "My mom will come first," I confidently announced to the others.

But she was not first. Feelings of fear began growing inside me as the other parents came and left with their children. Surely it wasn't long before my mom appeared, but it felt like forever to me. I don't remember the relief of her showing up as much as the fear she might not.

I shouldn't be surprised that my earliest memory as a child is connected to a fear. Science tells us that when a person experiences trauma, adrenaline and other neurochemicals rush to the brain and imprint a picture, a memory of what happened. And fear of abandonment is common for children to experience.

Now as an adult, I'd like to think I've learned to tame my fears with the strength of my faith. I've had plenty of practice with what I call "faith tests," which I believe God allows so we learn to make choices based on faith (truth) rather than fears (feelings). But I'm often a slow learner.

Just recently, a friend and I were having a casual conversation and realized we disagreed on a current controversial issue in our community. The power of my feelings surprised me as we voiced our differing opinions and then tried to gloss over the awkward ending. Driving home, I knew I could have handled the conversation better and I owed her an apology. But I dreaded the thought of revisiting the situation with her and slowly convinced myself it was fine to let it go.

Yet the next morning, the conviction of my faith brought me back to what I knew was true, that I did need to apologize to my friend. So I stepped over my fear and called her, and the feeling of relief was a blessing.

God's most repeated command in the Bible is "fear not." But faith tests are teaching me that often I have to just "do it scared."

The Bible is filled with examples of God's people overcoming their fears, standing on their faith. Doing it while being scared.

God told Moses to lead the Israelites out of Egypt, but they were pursued by angry Egyptians on fast horses. Imagine the Israelites' fears when they got to the edge of the Red Sea. God told Moses how to part the sea, but it took great faith for the Israelites to step onto the path of dry ground with huge walls of water on both sides. They had to trust God's provision. They had to step in and do it even though they were scared.

What I know to be true is that our smaller daily decisions to choose faith over fear prepare us for life's bigger fearful challenges. I lived through many small faith tests before facing the greatest challenge of my life.

We were on vacation in the Colorado mountains when my husband, Lynn, at age fifty-five, suddenly suffered a severe brain bleed and his life depended upon getting him to a brain surgeon on the other side of the mountains before it was too late. He was unconscious when he was lifted into a small plane. I climbed in by the pilot. Lynn was on a gurney in back, with a medic on either side. The line on the only monitor I could see fluctuated . . . and then flat-lined. I thought Lynn had died, especially because the medics wouldn't make eye contact with me, and the sound of the plane was too loud for conversation. I looked out the window at the snow-capped mountain peaks below and beautiful blue sky above and suddenly experienced a total sense of peace that passed all understanding. "Lord," I prayed, "if You have chosen to take Lynn here, thank You for this heavenly setting."

The plane landed, and one of the medics gave me a thumbs up as they quickly rolled Lynn into the hospital where a neuro-surgeon was waiting.

"Can you save him?" I frantically asked the doctor.

"I can keep his heart beating, but I don't know about his brain," he answered.

Hours later, the surgeon emerged to tell our gathered family that Lynn had survived the surgery, but his most critical challenges were ahead.

I felt overwhelmed by all the unknowns. A dear friend, who showed up at the hospital, took my hands and faced me, eye to eye. "Everything that has happened in your life until now has prepared you for what you are facing. Trust God and hold on to faith."

Her words reminded me of a scripture I'd often repeated about God's angel preparing the way on a fearful journey: "See, I am sending an angel ahead of you to guard you along the way and to bring you to the place I have prepared" (Exodus 23:20, NIV).

God's promises and my friend's words gave me strength through the long days Lynn was in a coma, followed by weeks of his slow progress in a rehab facility. Today, years later, Lynn and I continue our journey, trusting that God will prepare our way and give us what we need when we need it.

The book in your hands is filled with 100 devotions, personal stories of people just like you who have faced fears of all sizes and found comfort in God's words such as those found in Psalm 34:4 (NIV): "I sought the Lord, and he answered me; he delivered me from all my fears."

No matter where you place this book in your home, whether by your bed or on a table by a comfy chair, the message on the cover will continually remind you that faith over fear brings you rest in the shadow of His wings.

Practice Peacefulness

JOHN DILWORTH

Always be prepared to give an answer to everyone who asks you to give the reason for the hope that you have.

1 PETER 3:15 (NIV)

John, how do you always stay so calm, even in the tough situations?" a colleague asked.

I was sitting across the desk from the division president of my company for one last meeting. We were chatting, wrapping things up, before I formally retired. Not expecting the question, I rambled, mentioning my faith and that I hadn't always been calm. I talked about reading Dr. Norman Vincent Peale's books in my younger days and how they had helped me.

Later, I felt disappointed that my answer hadn't come close to capturing God's work within me to overcome the biggest struggle of my life: crippling fears and anxiety. I asked God to help me overcome all of my turmoil and inner conflict. I learned ways to live my faith. I began to pray and read the Bible daily. I used many of the action steps that Dr. Peale outlined to deal with daily life and to practice peacefulness. From that beginning, God guided me on an incredible journey, step by step, to a life of deep tranquility and quiet confidence.

I wasn't prepared to give an answer when the question was asked. I missed an opportunity to tell firsthand what God had done for me. However, the conversation may have been another step that God intended for my journey. It caused me to look back and see more clearly than ever His presence and faithfulness throughout my life—and that He is "the reason for the hope" I have.

Let Us Pray

Dear Lord, help me be ready to boldly share stories of Your faithfulness whenever an opportunity comes. Amen.

Further Reflection

1 CHRONICLES 16:9 (NIV)

Sing to him, sing praise to him; tell of all his wonderful acts.

PSALM 13:5–6 (NIV)

But I trust in your unfailing love; my heart rejoices in your salvation. I will sing the LORD's praise, for he has been good to me.

God's Got You

LOGAN ELIASEN

*But I trust in you, L*ORD*; I say,*
"You are my God."

PSALM 31:14 (NIV)

"Nice job, Logan!" my friend Steve shouted. "You're doing great!"

I looked down from the faux-stone wall I was clinging to. Steve was teaching me how to rock climb. He tightened the rope clipped to his waist. It connected to a pulley on the ceiling and down to my harness.

I was shaky from being so high up, but I also felt exhilarated. I swung my torso as I grasped for the next handhold, and I missed it. Suddenly, I was hanging from the rock face by one hand. I looked down at the gym floor, and my stomach clenched.

"It's OK, Logan!" Steve yelled. "That's why I'm here! You can let go now! I've got you!"

I was afraid. Instead of trusting Steve, I clawed and scrabbled to find a grip. *What if the rope isn't tight enough? What if it snaps? What if I weigh more than Steve and plummet to the floor while he rockets to the ceiling?*

I understood that I needed to release my grasp. But I struggle with surrender. I'm the firstborn of five, and I've got the personality that goes with it. Relying on myself feels safe and certain.

"Logan, you have to trust me," Steve said, calm and steady. That sounded very familiar. God also asks me to trust Him—to remember that He will keep me safe.

So now it was time to relinquish and release control instead of claw for it. I uncurled my fingers. I dropped, but the slack in the rope tightened. Then I hung, suspended peacefully in the air. Steve had expertly braced himself. He began to lower me to safety, and I breathed easy.

It's a good thing to be in capable hands—both Steve's and God's.

Let Us Pray

Lord, thank You for sending friends who teach me more about surrender and trust.

Further Reflection

PSALM 56:3 (NIV)

When I am afraid, I put my trust in you.

PROVERBS 3:5–6 (NIV)

Trust in the LORD with all your heart and lean not on your own understanding; in all your ways submit to him, and he will make your paths straight.

~ DEVOTION 3 ~

You Are Here

ERIN MacPHERSON

*On the day I called, you answered me;
my strength of soul you increased.*

PSALM 138:3 (ESV)

Just a little lump.

It's amazing how quickly life can shift out of orbit, how a mundane day can suddenly become anything but. All it takes is one fragment of a second when something just doesn't feel right.

Lord, why? How? my soul screams. I never imagined this for my dear friend Sarah.

Suddenly a whir of doctors' appointments and biopsies, of friends calling to give advice, of doctors calling to give results, of treatment calendars and care calendars and a chicken-poppy-seed casserole in the oven from the next-door neighbor as you hold hands and pray on the couch.

Big words like *cancer* and *chemotherapy* and *radiation* being tossed around like pinballs, big feelings creeping in and over-taking what was simply joy and peace only days ago. Yet You are here, Lord.

In those crazy, mixed-up moments when I don't know what to say or what to do or how to act other than to look my friend in her eyes and pull her close and hold on tight, You are here.

When she doesn't respond, when words can't be found, when the gap between us is bigger than it has ever been, You are here.

In sickness and in hope and tears and sweat and pain. In every moment, You are here. And in Your presence, peace flows.

Let Us Pray

Father God, thank You for comfort even in the midst of the hardest days. You are the strength I need when I have no strength to walk forward. Amen.

Further Reflection

ROMANS 8:16–17 (ESV)

The Spirit himself bears witness with our spirit that we are children of God, and if children, then heirs—heirs of God and fellow heirs with Christ, provided we suffer with him in order that we may also be glorified with him.

ROMANS 8:38–39 (ESV)

For I am sure that neither death nor life, nor angels nor rulers, nor things present nor things to come, nor powers, nor height nor depth, nor anything else in all creation, will be able to separate us from the love of God in Christ Jesus our Lord.

Love One Another

EDWARD GRINNAN

If it is possible, as far as it depends on you, live at peace with everyone.

ROMANS 12:18 (NIV)

I grew up in a politically aware family. Political arguments were a part of life in our household, especially between my liberal mom and my conservative dad. We debated everything and were never afraid to say what we believed, loudly and proudly. We subscribed to three daily newspapers and two news weeklies. My parents never went to bed until after the 11:00 p.m. local newscast.

Lately, though, our national discourse has grown increasingly rancorous, even toxic. People aren't just wrong or misguided—they're evil and nefarious. We vote our fears rather than our convictions.

How did we come to this? It's not altogether new. Jesus joined the human race at one of its great boiling points. Jerusalem was a hotbed of political strife. Imperial Rome was an oppressive occupier of Jewish lands and ruled from afar with a merciless hand. Herod and his family were ruthless and corrupt. Revolution was in the air, and violence was never far. Nazareth was poor and overpopulated and crime-ridden. The Zealots were already plotting insurrection.

It was into this roiling political cauldron that Jesus deliberately came, having planned to come at this exact moment since

the very beginning of time. His message of peace for all human-kind was a rank political contradiction. His command to love one another was a historical absurdity.

Yet it was the message that endured through the ages, the gospel of love and not hate, of peace and not strife. The word of Jesus still prevails, then as now. I have to listen closely to hear the eternal message of a peace that surpasses all understanding.

Let Us Pray

God, Your peace is beyond human comprehension. Teach us not to hate but to disagree as brothers and sisters, not enemies.

Further Reflection

1 PETER 3:8–9 (NIV)

Finally, all of you, be like-minded, be sympathetic, love one another, be compassionate and humble. Do not repay evil with evil or insult with insult. On the contrary, repay evil with blessing, because to this you were called so that you may inherit a blessing.

In God's Hands Now

MARCI ALBORGHETTI

I know, O LORD, that the way of human beings is not in their control, that mortals as they walk cannot direct their steps.

JEREMIAH 10:23 (NRSV)

In the mirror, my husband's eyes were red-rimmed, his brow creased. And to say that about Charlie is indeed saying something distressing. He is the most optimistic, affable, easygoing person in any room.

In the emergency room after my fall, I'd watched Charlie beg an orderly to give me pain medication, only to be told that we'd have to wait for the doctor. He dashed back and forth, as near to panic as I'd ever seen him.

"Well," the doctor began grimly, when he came in holding the X-rays, "you really did a job." Broken collarbone. Cracked rib. Deep tissue bruising. I was warned against puncturing a lung.

Now, twenty-four hours later, a good part of me was purple with lines of red and yellow. Charlie and I surveyed the damage in the mirror. He clasped my right hand. I began to cry. A week ago, we'd renewed our vows and planned daily workout walks, activities with our godsons, and travel.

"Nothing will ever be the same," I said, choking up. Even sobbing hurt.

"That's not true. Don't say that," Charlie pleaded, and then his face crumpled.

Charlie's unique combination of charm, intelligence, and kindness has accustomed him to easily getting and maintaining control. While I constantly battle myself to acknowledge that God is in charge, Charlie quite contentedly assumes that God wants him to take control.

But now *neither* of us had it.

When I saw Charlie's face fall, God gave me new words: "We're in God's hands now. We've always been, but now we know it." Charlie's fingers tightened on mine.

Let Us Pray

Lord, let me release my pain and sin to
You and not burden others.

Further Reflection

MATTHEW 4:15–16 (NRSV)

Land of Zebulun, land of Naphtali, on the road by the sea, across the Jordan, Galilee of the gentiles—the people who sat in darkness have seen a great light, and for those who sat in the region and shadow of death light has dawned.

~ DEVOTION 6 ~

Be Prepared

RHODA BLECKER

Fear not, Abram, I am a shield to you.

GENESIS 15:1 (JPS)

The Northridge earthquake, whose epicenter was less than a mile from our house, had been pretty terrifying. So when *The New Yorker* published its Pulitzer Prize–winning article on the peril to those of us living in the Cascadia earthquake zone, a lot of people here in the Pacific Northwest got nervous. After all, the prospect of a serious quake and perhaps a tsunami was scary. I expected to be one of the frightened.

But, strangely, I wasn't. When my husband, Keith, and I lived in Los Angeles, preparation for a quake was a given. After the Sylmar quake, the earliest one I'd experienced, I learned to keep supplies of water and food and to anchor pictures to the walls with Velcro. When we moved into our house in the San Fernando Valley, we went further than that. Every piece of furniture taller than I am was strapped to the walls, all the knick-knacks were fastened down with museum wax, and we kept a crowbar and a short-handled sledgehammer under the side of our bed.

Those preparations helped protect us when Northridge happened. In spite of the months of necessary repair and recovery, we were unhurt. That experience gave me confidence that God had seen us through, demonstrating to us in unmistakable

14

terms that He was with us when the ground shook and anything not tied down crashed to the floor. I believe that, even if Cascadia were to break loose in my lifetime, as long as I keep faith and prepare, He might well see fit to bring me through again.

Let Us Pray

Please be a shield to me, too, God of Abraham, just as You were my protector in the past.

Further Reflection

PROVERBS 1:33 (JPS)

But whoso hearkeneth unto me shall dwell securely, And shall be quiet without fear of evil.

ISAIAH 48:17 (JPS)

Thus saith the LORD, thy Redeemer, The Holy One of Israel: I am the LORD thy God, Who teacheth thee for thy profit, Who leadeth thee by the way that thou shouldest go.

Have Confidence

SHARON FOSTER

*Ye are the light of the world. A city
that is set on a hill cannot be hid.*

MATTHEW 5:14 (KJV)

Before I became a writer, I instructed military personnel on how to teach—presentation skills, lesson plan writing, and evaluation methods. It was a joy to help fearless warriors overcome their fear of public speaking so they could inspire others. I told them, "Risk doing more than you think you can; your students are hungry to hear what you have to say."

But I understood their fear. When I was just beginning to put pen to paper, I struggled to find the confidence and courage to write. It made me feel vulnerable. I bargained with God: *I will write for You, Lord, but let me keep my privacy.*

Two years later, I was sitting next to my cousin, who is also my best friend, at a conference attended by over ten thousand women. As a newly published author, my confidence about being a writer was still fragile. But at the conference, I was full of joy. Only the pastor leading the conference, his wife, and my cousin knew me. I embraced my anonymity.

Suddenly, I saw the pastor walking in my direction, his hand extended toward me. He was going to introduce me to an international audience. I panicked! I shook my head, silently pleading with the pastor to leave me in peace. He honored my plea.

Recently, I've considered what an opportunity I missed to impact the kingdom. Maybe it was because I was raised in the sixties as the only girl in my family. My wonderful parents had their hands full, pushing my four brothers forward while at the same time trying to keep me docile and ladylike.

For years, I ignored my failure during that event. But no more, Lord. I'm going to let my light shine!

Let Us Pray

Lord, forgive my fear. Forgive me for rebuffing You and the pastor. Use me, Lord! Help me not to fear being a light in this world.

Further Reflection

JOHN 12:36 (NKJV)

"While you have the light, believe in the light, that you may become sons of light." These things Jesus spoke, and departed, and was hidden from them.

JOHN 21:17 (NKJV)

He said to him the third time, "Simon, son of Jonah, do you love Me?" Peter was grieved because He said to him the third time, "Do you love Me?" And he said to Him, "Lord, You know all things; You know that I love You." Jesus said to him, "Feed My sheep."

Step Outside Your Comfort Zone

PATRICIA LORENZ

*Don't be impatient. Wait for the Lord,
and he will come and save you! Be brave,
stouthearted, and courageous. Yes,
wait and he will help you.*

PSALM 27:14 (TLB)

On a warm, sunny February day in Florida, I was visiting Sawgrass Lake Park. Walking on the boardwalk above the natural Florida ferns, oaks, and swampy areas, I came upon a 10-foot-long alligator and about twenty little ones from 6 inches to 2 feet in length. That big old mama gator did not move an inch, nor did she even open her eyes as I stood on the boardwalk just 3 feet above her. Mama gator looked so peaceful and content, surrounded by her numerous babies from different litters. Some had been born just a month earlier, others a year or two earlier. I felt perfectly safe because the boardwalk has a 3-foot-high railing of vertical boards on both sides.

When I texted my twelve-year-old granddaughter, Adeline, who lives in California, about my gator encounter, she replied, "Oh, I would never be able to go anywhere like that if alligators were there." I reassured her it was perfectly safe because of the enclosed boardwalk and that I would take her there when she came to visit to see for herself.

Adeline attended an art school in downtown Oakland, where she often navigated on her own by public transportation. To her, it's nothing. To me, with my small-town upbringing and small-town life now, I would be uncomfortable trying to find my way around in a big city like Oakland by myself, especially at night. After my conversation with Adeline, I understood that each of us has fears that can easily be evaporated by taking on the world and perhaps holding hands with the one I love while I experience something outside my comfort zone. Oakland, here I come!

Let Us Pray

Father, You gave us an amazing world with incredible adventures and creatures and places to experience. Be with me and calm my heart as I step out to explore Your world.

Further Reflection

1 CHRONICLES 22:13 (TLB)

For if you carefully obey the rules and regulations that he gave to Israel through Moses, you will prosper. Be strong and courageous, fearless and enthusiastic!

1 CHRONICLES 28:20 (TLB)

Then he continued, "Be strong and courageous and get to work. Don't be frightened by the size of the task, for the Lord my God is with you; he will not forsake you. He will see to it that everything is finished correctly."

The Gift of Love

PAM KIDD

My heart was grieved.

PSALM 73:21 (NKJV)

"Y ou have to come right now," my niece Michele sobbed. Standing in the mall, I held my phone tightly and hung the shirt back on the rack. "What's wrong, Michele?" But I knew, though my heart was begging me not to know. My brother was dying.

We had been with him three days before. He seemed on the way back from a terrible bout with cancer. He and my husband, David, were talking of fishing; a trip to Tellico, our father's birthplace; and, best of all, his reconciliation and anticipated remarriage to his first wife, Carol, mother of his daughters, Kristi and Michele.

I had always adored my big brother Davey. He was the smartest student in every class, gentle and sweet, every teacher's favorite. He loved baseball, especially the Chattanooga Lookouts, and always had his glove primed, ready to catch that elusive fly ball at game time.

Recently, I had texted him: "I can see us at our little table, eating alphabet soup or peanut butter and banana mixed for lunch. Safe and happy and cared for. I've never met anyone who had a better childhood. Nothing on this earth can touch it."

"I think about that too," he texted back, "and I totally agree. I never realized at the time just how unique and perfect it was."

Davey never caught the fly ball. His most recent plans didn't happen. But he had gone to God in peace with his family reunited around him.

At the end of our last visit, Davey had pulled me close and, totally out of character, he had whispered in my ear, "I love you."

"I love you back," I said.

I'll always grieve for Davey. But the happy times make it easy to let go of regrets. His last gift of "I love you" moves me toward tomorrow with joy.

Let Us Pray

Father, in our grief, help us remember love
in whatever way it has been offered to us.

Further Reflection

PSALM 30:5 (NKJV)

For His anger is but for a moment, His favor is for life; weeping may endure for a night, but joy comes in the morning.

ISAIAH 53:4 (NKJV)

Surely He has borne our griefs and carried our sorrows; yet we esteemed Him stricken, smitten by God, and afflicted.

Listen for the Whistle

LOGAN ELIASEN

When Moses' hands grew tired, they took a stone and put it under him and he sat on it. Aaron and Hur held his hands up—one on one side, one on the other—so that his hands remained steady till sunset.

EXODUS 17:12 (NIV)

I ran my fingers through my beard and fidgeted with my graduation cap. Three more names, and then I would walk onstage.

Logan Eliasen, Juris Doctor.

I didn't know if it was the thought of acquiring that title or the fact that I was wearing three layers of clothing that made me break out into a sweat. Was I ready to practice law—to carry the weight of defending other people's rights and livelihoods?

The line moved forward, but I was looking backward. I wanted to return to being a student, where the only person I was responsible for was myself. The past looked easier, more comfortable. For a moment, I stood in the dark. My robes blended into the backstage shadows.

"Logan Eliasen," the announcer called, breaking me from my thoughts. I stepped tentatively onto the bright stage. I looked out over the crowd. The jumble of faces made my throat tighten. I didn't recognize anybody.

Then a whistle pierced through the silence and broke through my uncertainty. My mom's whistle. The same one that had cheered me on since Little League. And that whistle was followed by cheers and shouts—the rest of my family.

I knew that I was going to be all right because people who loved me were on my side. And they would continue to strengthen and support me as I moved forward into my career as a lawyer.

The shouts and clapping continued as I received my diploma and shook hands with the dean. And as I exited the other side of the stage, my mom's whistle followed me.

Let Us Pray

Father, thank You for providing people
to hold me up when I am unsteady.

Further Reflection

ECCLESIASTES 4:9–10 (NIV)

Two are better than one, because they have a good return for their labor: if either of them falls down, one can help the other up. But pity anyone who falls and has no one to help them up.

1 THESSALONIANS 5:11 (NIV)

Therefore encourage one another and build each other up, just as in fact you are doing.

Stop Pretending

ERIN JANOSO

I prayed to the LORD, and he answered me.
He freed me from all my fears.

PSALM 34:4 (NLT)

I gripped my armrest as our plane lurched suddenly up and then down. The seatbelt light dinged overhead. I glanced over to check my five-year-old daughter's belt.

"Ooh Mom!" she said. "That was fun!"

I smiled at her, remembering how, not that long ago, even the slightest turbulence would send me into panic mode.

I hadn't always been afraid of flying. As a child, I remembered enjoying it, as Aurora was now. But somewhere along the way, fear crept in. When flying, and honestly, in most other things too, worrying felt like something I could *do* to help keep us safe. It was as though I was showing God I knew how fragile my life was.

My husband opened my eyes to the folly of this idea. "You focus on outcomes opposite of the ones you're praying for," he pointed out. He was right. I prayed fervently to God to keep us safe and then spent the rest of every flight sure we would crash. Where was the faith in that? So I changed my airplane prayers. I still asked for safety. But I started asking for help with my fear as well. When things got bumpy, I stopped indulging in thoughts of catastrophe, and I worked hard to at least pretend my stomach wasn't in my throat.

Eventually, I realized I wasn't pretending as often. Those menacing bumps and shudders weren't as terrifying as they'd once been. I still didn't like turbulence, but I no longer believed it meant a crash was imminent.

Our plane shook again, and Aurora patted her tummy, a big grin on her face. "These bumps tickle!" she said.

"They kinda do, don't they?" I answered, and we laughed together.

Let Us Pray

Thank You, Lord, for showing me that You are the conqueror of all my fears.

Further Reflection

MATTHEW 6:27 (NLT)

Can all your worries add a single moment to your life?

2 CORINTHIANS 12:9 (NLT)

Each time he said, "My grace is all you need. My power works best in weakness." So now I am glad to boast about my weaknesses, so that the power of Christ can work through me.

Worst-Case Scenario

EDWARD GRINNAN

*May the God of hope fill you with all
joy and peace as you trust in him, so that
you may overflow with hope by
the power of the Holy Spirit.*

ROMANS 15:13 (NIV)

It was one of the hardest decisions of our thirty-three-year
marriage. We'd both avoided it, especially Julee, but her
suffering had grown unbearable, the disks in her spinal column
being crushed by damaged vertebrae. Finally, she was willing to
take a chance on surgery.

She'd injured her back during years as a singer and actress.
Once, performing a concert in Bucharest, she tripped over a
cable as she was coming onstage and nearly had to cancel the
performance. As it was, she could barely move during that
show. In a crazy off-Broadway musical when we were first
married, her role required her to be hoisted aloft to escape a
space monster (I kid you not). The hoist operator was new and
wrenched Julee's back out of alignment.

She'd tried everything for relief: injections, pills, physical
therapy, yoga, massage, meditation, rest—lots and lots of rest.
Finally, reluctantly, she had agreed to surgery, even if it would
have to wait a bit due to a flare-up of her lupus.

"Edward, I'm scared."

"I know, baby, but the doctor says the risks are minimal. The worst-case scenario is you stay the same."

"That's what scares me. Staying the same. That's the same as losing hope, and I can't lose hope."

She was right. What outcome could be worse than the loss of hope? Of knowing nothing will change? I'm not sure I could face that risk. But Julee will. She told me, "There's only one way I can do this: with God. I don't ask Him to take away the fear, just to go through it with me."

I'll be there for Julee, and will also ask God to be there for both of us.

Let Us Pray

Father in heaven, in our deepest pain,
we turn to You for hope.

Further Reflection

ROMANS 5:2–5 (NIV)

. . . through whom we have gained access by faith into this grace in which we now stand. And we boast in the hope of the glory of God. Not only so, but we also glory in our sufferings, because we know that suffering produces perseverance; perseverance, character; and character, hope. And hope does not put us to shame, because God's love has been poured out into our hearts through the Holy Spirit, who has been given to us.

ROMANS 8:25 (NIV)

But if we hope for what we do not yet have, we wait for it patiently.

The Big Oak Tree

ERIN MacPHERSON

Whatever you ask in my name,
this I will do, that the Father may be
glorified in the Son. If you ask me
anything in my name, I will do it.

JOHN 14:13–14 (ESV)

We planned to meet under the big oak tree to pray for Sarah. It was still early after her diagnosis, and only a few of us knew the battle she was facing. We knew that within the week, letters would be sent, a port would scar her chest, her hair would begin to fall out.

We knew that without God, none of us would survive the coming months.

And so we met under that tree, leaves blowing down from waving branches, our hands clasping each other's, our faces streaming with tears. And we prayed that God would take this burden from Sarah, that she would be miraculously healed, that He would get all of the glory.

There was a moment when the hand grasping mine clenched a bit tighter and I looked up to see tears, eyes full of desperation. Every woman in that circle paused. Considered. Swallowed hard.

And then the terrifying, hopeful words were said: not our wills but His alone.

And so our prayers changed. We prayed that God would fill us with peace and hope regardless of the circumstances; that He would surround Sarah, her husband, her children, and us with His unfailing, undying, undiminishing love; that our wills would align with His; that we would be able to rely unwaveringly on Him.

Let Us Pray

Lord, Your love is revealed to us every day,
both in joyful moments and in painful situations.
Thank You. Amen.

Further Reflection

The Rock, his work is perfect, for all his ways are justice. A God of faithfulness and without iniquity, just and upright is he.

The LORD is near to all who call on him, to all who call on him in truth.

God Is Near

SCOTT WALKER

I fear no evil; for thou art with me.

PSALM 23:4 (RSV)

I once read that anxiety is the human condition. After living six decades, I know this is true. Though I may appear confident, uncertainty and fear often grip me. A close friend was critically injured, and I feared for his life. My wife, Beth, and I attended her forty-fifth high school reunion. It was a wonderful time of greeting old classmates, but we were grateful for name tags with large, legible print. Then we learned our son Drew and his wife, Katie Alice, were expecting a daughter. We were ecstatic, but we were also fearful for Katie Alice's health, the baby's health, and on and on.

One weekend, when Beth and I escaped to a favorite cottage on the Florida coast, I took a long walk on the beach. It was near midnight, and the moon was full and the stars brilliant. I gazed into the vast darkness and found myself thinking, *Is God real or just a myth? Is eternity a wonderful new dimension of unimagined experience or is death merely extinction?* I prayed that

I would see my unborn granddaughter reach her wedding day. Amid the beauty, thoughts pounded me. I felt tense and tentative.

As I walked, I heard the Psalmist's calm voice: "The Lord is my shepherd, I shall not want. . . . Even though I walk through the valley of the shadow of death, I fear no evil; for thou art with me. . . . Surely goodness and mercy shall follow me all the days of my life; and I shall dwell in the house of the Lord for ever" (Psalm 23:1, 4, 6, RSV).

Slowly the rhythm of the surf embraced me. I knew that the God of holy mystery was near. And I was no longer afraid.

Let Us Pray

**Father, help me accept my anxious nature
and follow You. Amen.**

Further Reflection

JOHN 10:11–14 (RSV)

I am the good shepherd. The good shepherd lays down his life for the sheep. He who is a hireling and not a shepherd, whose own the sheep are not, sees the wolf coming and leaves the sheep and flees; and the wolf snatches them and scatters them. He flees because he is a hireling and cares nothing for the sheep. I am the good shepherd; I know my own and my own know me.

Try Not to Worry

JULIE GARMON

Surely the LORD is in this place.

GENESIS 28:16 (NIV)

After a routine blood draw, I received an unsettling phone call from my doctor. "Mrs. Garmon, you're severely anemic. You need to see your gastroenterologist to make sure you're not bleeding internally." Although she spoke in a gentle tone, I could hear the concern in her voice.

My gastroenterologist fit me in quickly, ordered more blood work, and prescribed iron. "We need to do a colonoscopy to rule out cancer." Her pale blue eyes locked with mine. "I'd like to wait until your iron level increases, but that's a bit risky." She smiled. "Try not to worry."

I refused all fear until the morning of my procedure. Then, lying on a gurney, awaiting anesthesia, I wondered, *Is it possible not to be afraid?* Worst-case-scenario thinking had plagued me for most of my life, and being put to sleep had always been particularly scary for me. In the past, I had shaken so violently, my teeth would chatter.

No telling what the doctor might find, I thought. A couple of tremors ran through me. *Oh no, not again. Fear is so exhausting.*

"They're ready for you," a nurse said and wheeled me back.

Waiting for my anesthesia, a thought so astounding came to me that I laughed.

"What's so funny?" the nurse said. "I love good jokes."

"Something just dawned on me: I can't perform my own colonoscopy or control the results, so I might as well relax."

She patted my hand. "We'll take good care of you. God will too."

The most peaceful feeling enfolded me; all of the shaking ceased. I knew "surely the Lord is in this place."

Let Us Pray

Father, no shaking, no fear! Thank You.

Further Reflection

PSALM 115:11 (NIV)

You who fear him, trust in the LORD—he is their help and shield.

PSALM 118:6 (NIV)

The LORD is with me; I will not be afraid. What can mere mortals do to me?

Blessed Assurance

MARION BOND WEST

Even the darkness will not be dark to you; the night will shine like the day, for darkness is as light to you.

PSALM 139:12 (NIV)

Taking the trash out," my husband, Gene, called to me. He rolled the large container to the curb every Wednesday night. I was absorbed in a book. Maybe twelve minutes passed. Suddenly, I looked up and missed him. As I hurried out the garage door, I heard him bellowing, "Over here, hurry." Even at night, I managed to see him lying on the ground. As I knelt by him, he said grimly, "I think I've broken my hip. Call an ambulance."

I flew back inside to grab my cell phone and coat. Back at his side, I eased my lap underneath his head and threw the coat over him. Then I dialed the dreaded 911. When the ambulance arrived, one of the EMTs said, "It's gonna hurt, sir. But we'll try to be gentle."

Gene groaned loudly as they lifted him. The red lights of the ambulance flashed rapidly; I was still wearing my fuzzy bedroom slippers. The entire scene seemed unreal, and, in a moment, our quiet lives had changed. Fear was slipping up behind me. I couldn't form words to pray.

Just then, I glanced upward as the back doors of the emergency vehicle shut with Gene inside. *Oh my!* How bright the night was. Stars twinkling as only stars can, a glimmering moon, and black velvet sky—the exact same brilliant sky I'd gazed up at as a child lying on a quilt in my front yard.

Lingering for just a moment longer, I inhaled deeply as though breathing in some kind of blessed assurance given off by the startling beauty of the heavens. God was there just as always. I knew He saw us and would go through whatever lies ahead with us.

Let Us Pray

Thank You, Father, for all the ambulances You ride in.

Further Reflection

MALACHI 3:6 (NIV)

I the LORD do not change. So you, the descendants of Jacob, are not destroyed.

Trust Others

ANDREW ATTAWAY

For ye are all the children of God by faith in Christ Jesus. For as many of you as have been baptized into Christ have put on Christ.

GALATIANS 3:26–27 (KJV)

For the past four years, I've been getting treatment for my depression at a clinic. The clinic has many advantages: it's close to home, it has a great staff and facilities, and we can afford it. But it has a downside too. Since it's a training clinic, doctors rotate in and out every two years.

I've developed a very good relationship with my therapist for the last two years. I've been able to go with him into the most painful and problematic parts of my life. I trust him. It's hard to establish that kind of trust, and I was worried about having to start the whole process again.

Trusting people enough to share my heart with them isn't easy for me. I'm afraid that if I let them see through the public me, then the private me will repel them. It's not a rational response, I know; it's an automatic emotional reaction that's very hard for me to work through.

Unfortunately, my difficulties with trust aren't confined to other people; they get in the way of my relationship with God too. Over and over again, scripture urges us to trust the Lord. There's no false front I can put up to fool God; whether I like it or not, He can see right through me. And that's pretty scary.

These verses from Galatians help me see past the fear. When I came to Christ, I put on Christ. And when the Father looks at me, it's not my sins and inadequacies He sees; it's His Son, who has taken them up and clothed them with Himself. That's where I should be looking too.

Let Us Pray

Lord Jesus Christ, teach me how to trust in You.

Further Reflection

PSALM 33:21 (KJV)

For our heart shall rejoice in him, because we have trusted in his holy name.

PROVERBS 3:5 (KJV)

Trust in the Lord with all thine heart; and lean not unto thine own understanding.

1 TIMOTHY 1:14 (KJV)

And the grace of our Lord was exceeding abundant with faith and love which is in Christ Jesus.

Balance the Load

DANIEL SCHANTZ

The LORD is my helper; I will not fear.
What can man do to me?

HEBREWS 13:6 (NKJV)

I awake with a pounding heart and a sense of dread. I have a doctor's appointment this afternoon. "Lord, help me face this day," I pray. Maybe some doughnuts from the bakery will cheer me, but when I twist the ignition key, the car won't start. *Oh, great. Just what I need. Something else to worry about!*

I do my own repairs, so I am soon up to my elbows in tools and test instruments. I feel like Sherlock Holmes probing for that one elusive clue that will unravel this mystery. I enjoy removing parts and discovering the engine's deepest secrets. It feels masculine tugging hard on wrenches, stretching my arm muscles. I twist and bend, looking for concealed bolt heads. Soon I am breathing hard, but it's stimulating, refreshing.

Then comes that eureka moment: *It's the coolant temperature sensor! A cheap, easy fix!* An hour later, I turn the key and the engine fires to life. I feel a huge sense of conquest, man over machine. I am John Henry, the steel-driving man!

I am grinning from ear to ear when my wife opens the kitchen door. "It's time for lunch. And don't forget, you have a doctor's appointment."

I did forget! So absorbed was I in my work that there was no room for anxiety.

The appointment went all right, and on the way home, I gave myself a lecture. "Next time you are facing a threat, find something to occupy your mind. If not car repair, then gardening or helping Sharon clean house."

Just as it's easier to carry two suitcases than one to balance the load, sometimes one problem can balance out another. Thank You, God, for keeping me balanced in my time of fear.

Let Us Pray

Lord, I am embarrassed to be so afraid of doctors, but thank You for helping me to manage my fears.

Further Reflection

DEUTERONOMY 20:1 (NKJV)

When you go out to battle against your enemies, and see horses and chariots and people more numerous than you, do not be afraid of them; for the LORD your God is with you, who brought you up from the land of Egypt.

2 KINGS 6:16 (NKJV)

So he answered, "Do not fear, for those who are with us are more than those who are with them."

Grab the Essentials

ASHLEY KAPPEL

Guard against every kind of greed. Life is not measured by how much you own.

LUKE 12:15 (NLT)

Alabama is full of wonderful things: gorgeous beaches, the last foothills of the Appalachians, and more barbecue than is reasonable for anyone to consume. But it also comes with its moments of panic, especially in April, which is the start of tornado season.

This part of the country calls itself the "Buckle of the Bible Belt." Though it has a lot of faith, it also has a lot of fear, as evidenced by the absence of bread, milk, and water in the grocery store every time the siren sounds for incoming dangerous weather.

Last April, it was just my husband, Brian, our golden retriever, Colby, and me hunkering down in our basement for a few nights. We slept soundly, huddled in our warm blankets.

Now that I'm a mom with a one-year-old, this April feels very different when the siren sounds. There's more urgency, more of an edge to how I feel, knowing that I have to wake little Olivia sleeping in her crib so that we can seek safety from the storm.

As we prepare to head downstairs, I begin to play that childhood game: if I had to suddenly dash for shelter, what three things would I grab? In the past, I'd thought about photos, documents, and letters Brian had written to me in college. But this time, I look at my sleeping daughter, my gentle dog, and my wonderful husband and feel my fear dissipate. Everything that matters is already gathered close around me.

Let Us Pray

Lord, when You blessed me with family, You gave new meaning to my true life. Help me to remember that we are safe in Your care always.

Further Reflection

MATTHEW 8:24–26 (NLT)

Suddenly, a fierce storm struck the lake, with waves breaking into the boat. But Jesus was sleeping. The disciples went and woke him up, shouting, "Lord, save us! We're going to drown!" Jesus responded, "Why are you afraid? You have so little faith!" Then he got up and rebuked the wind and waves, and suddenly there was a great calm.

No Leaks

BILL GIOVANNETTI

*Don't worry about anything; instead, pray
about everything. Tell God what you need,
and thank him for all he has done.*

PHILIPPIANS 4:6 (NLT)

There was a knock at the door at 7:00 in the morning. Thinking that only an emergency can cause someone to knock on the door this early, I sprinted to see who was there. My neighbor Jack was trying to catch his breath. "Bill, your water main sprung a leak! It's gushing down the hillside!"

I jumped into action. Our house sits on top of a hill, higher than the municipal water supply. A pump pushes the water uphill to our house. That pump sits about a block away, near the base of the hill and right above Jack's house. I could picture gushing water flooding his beautiful home.

My first *action* was to throw tools into my car. My first *reaction* was fear. *What if I can't fix it? What if the pump blew? What if it's expensive? What if I damage my neighbor's house? What if I don't know what to do?* I said an emergency prayer: "Lord, help!"

I arrived at the pump to see a massive flood from a cracked pipe. The good news was it was from the supply side, meaning my pump was OK. The bad news was I'd have to shut off my water to stop it.

Fortunately, my neighbor's house had no damage, and I could fix the broken PVC pipes. I calmed down and figured out what I had to do and what parts I had to buy. After three trips to the hardware store and eight hours of digging, cutting, gluing, waiting, sweating, and praying, I turned the water main back on.

No leaks.

God treats me better than I deserve.

Let Us Pray

Thank You, Father, for strengthening me through life's stressful moments.

Further Reflection

PSALM 27:13–14 (NLT)

Yet I am confident I will see the LORD's goodness while I am here in the land of the living. Wait patiently for the LORD. Be brave and courageous. Yes, wait patiently for the LORD.

1 PETER 5:7 (NLT)

Give all your worries and cares to God, for he cares about you.

What Really Matters

ROBERTA MESSNER

Your adornment must not be merely external . . . but it should be the hidden person of the heart.

1 PETER 3:3–4 (NASB)

I looked in the magnifying mirror, and my face didn't look the same. It wasn't anything I could put my finger on, but I telephoned my doctor. "Why don't you come in this afternoon and we'll have a look?" he said.

The moment my doctor saw me, his demeanor became frantic. "I'm wondering if maybe we should have drained that hematoma in the beginning," he said. "Sometimes things like this can cause a person's face to disintegrate. I fear that's what is happening to you."

"Is it reversible?" I asked, my voice shaking, panicky.

"Not always."

Right away, I made plans to see my surgeon at the Cleveland Clinic. "The trauma of your fall has caused your tumor to return," he told me. "We can only hope this won't progress with a vengeance."

"When can we remove the growth?" I demanded.

"We can't." He rubbed his cheek and then patted my shoulder. "The new tumor is too close to the facial nerve. We can't take a chance on severing it." His eyes met mine. "But, really, your eyeglasses camouflage most of the disfigurement."

His physician's assistant chimed in, "And you're quite beautiful, in spite of this. Inside and out."

What reassuring words! I'm beautiful. Inside and out. Thank You, God, for friends who see all of me.

Let Us Pray

Oh, Lord, let me seek the kind of beauty You desire!

Further Reflection

GENESIS 1:31 (NASB)

And God saw all that He had made, and behold, it was very good. And there was evening and there was morning, the sixth day.

EZEKIEL 28:17 (NASB)

Your heart was haughty because of your beauty; you corrupted your wisdom by reason of your splendor.
I threw you to the ground; I put you before kings, that they may see you.

MATTHEW 23:27 (NASB)

Woe to you, scribes and Pharisees, hypocrites! For you are like whitewashed tombs which on the outside appear beautiful, but inside they are full of dead men's bones and all uncleanness.

The Ultimate Ending

CAROL KUYKENDALL

He has risen from the dead. . . .
Now I have told you.

MATTHEW 28:7 (NIV)

I went into the kitchen after a restless night, thinking about a friend recently diagnosed with a brain tumor considered terminal, and turned on the morning news. A man had just hijacked a car with a four-year-old boy inside. Police were chasing the driver through the streets of Denver in rush-hour traffic. A helicopter was filming the pursuit live, showing the car going eighty miles per hour through red lights and busy intersections.

I watched in horror, waiting for the accident that was sure to happen. Amazingly, this car kept missing others. The chase went on for ten minutes with dangerous maneuvers across an open field to access another busy highway, where the man drove the wrong way. Finally, he got a flat tire and the car spun to a stop. The suspect jumped out and started running, but police surrounded him. The chase was over. I felt exhausted but relieved that it ended safely, especially for the child in the back seat.

Later, I watched a rerun of the shocking events with my husband but was surprised to find that it was a totally different emotional experience for me. I felt no fear because I knew the end of the story.

I kept thinking about the parallel of the car chase to my friend's cancer diagnosis. Even as her story unfolds with frightening unknowns, I know the ultimate ending. God promises us eternal life. My friend knows that promise, too, and I can pray she keeps receiving comfort in believing.

Let Us Pray

Lord, You have already written the ending, which gives us hope while still living in the middle of our stories.

Further Reflection

LUKE 24:1–8 (NIV)

On the first day of the week, very early in the morning, the women took the spices they had prepared and went to the tomb. They found the stone rolled away from the tomb, but when they entered, they did not find the body of the Lord Jesus. While they were wondering about this, suddenly two men in clothes that gleamed like lightning stood beside them. In their fright the women bowed down with their faces to the ground, but the men said to them, "Why do you look for the living among the dead? He is not here; he has risen! Remember how he told you, while he was still with you in Galilee: 'The Son of Man must be delivered over to the hands of sinners, be crucified and on the third day be raised again.'" Then they remembered his words.

His Sanctuary

JULIE GARMON

*Worship the L*ord *with gladness.*

PSALM 100:2 (NIV)

My mind was far from worshipping God. I'd learned that a project I'd been working on needed major changes. I had no idea how to begin. I wasn't even sure I wanted to. I felt stupid, incapable, exhausted.

My husband, Rick, and I found our usual seats at church. When the praise music began, I was a million miles away, thinking, worrying, pouting, doubting. I mumbled the words to the song and faked my way through the second one. Before the final song, the worship leader said, "If you're comfortable doing this, let's try something new. Place your hand over your heart as we sing this next song."

Oh, great. I don't want to. Maybe no one else will either.

The worship leader's voice softened. "I want us to draw near to God. He is worthy of our worship. He is holy. He longs to hear our praise in His sanctuary." Then the pianist began playing. "Holy Spirit, Thou art welcome in this place . . ."

The words filled the sanctuary, and the music lifted high above our heads toward heaven. I could see hundreds of people slipping their hands over their hearts, even Rick. They weren't following directions because they had to; they wanted to.

Forgive me, Lord, I prayed silently.

I raised my right hand and covered my heart. The very instant I let go of my will and praised Him in His sanctuary, my spirit connected with His. All heaviness, fear, and doubt left me. With His help, I'd face my fears head-on.

Let Us Pray

"Holy Spirit, Thou art welcome in
this place and in my heart."

Further Reflection

JOHN 4:23 (NIV)

Yet a time is coming and has now come when the true worshipers will worship the Father in the Spirit and in truth, for they are the kind of worshipers the Father seeks.

ANTs

KAREN BARBER

*As water wears away stones and
torrents wash away the soil, so you
destroy a person's hope.*

JOB 14:19 (NIV)

*T*hings will never change and get better.

This seemed to be my recurring thought during a dark time in my life. I put on the outward appearance of everything being OK, but inside I felt paralyzed by worry and fear. Nothing seemed to help.

Then, one day, I attended a talk by a counselor who explained something that psychologists call automatic negative thoughts (ANTs). He said that without realizing it, ANTs spontaneously come into our minds and we believe them because we've thought them for so long. He went on to say that people can be taught to question the truth of these thoughts in order to get their thinking unstuck.

At home, I sat down with my journal and wrote myself a question: "What is my biggest fear today?" Right away, I wrote

down, "That things will never get better with a problem at church and with our son Chris." Next, I wrote, "See what words are crushing hope." I looked back at my statement and circled the word *never*.

I thought for a moment and wrote, "I challenge the word *never* by asking God to show me one way that each of these situations has actually improved." The next thing I knew, I had written down two small ways that each one seemed a little better. Then I wrote down an affirmation: "With Your help, O God, progress can be made and is being made."

Now when negativity invades my thoughts, I look to this affirmation—and God, who never crushes hope.

Let Us Pray

Dear Holy Spirit, I challenge these ANTs by holding them up to You. Amen.

Further Reflection

PSALM 119:116 (NIV)

Sustain me, my God, according to your promise, and I will live; do not let my hopes be dashed.

Don't Forget Your Dreams

RICK HAMLIN

Jesus went down to Nazareth with them and was obedient to them. His mother cherished every word in her heart.

LUKE 2:51 (CEB)

Oh, what hopes we have for our children, what dreams! Both of our sons were born in winter, and I can remember during Advent, when Carol was "great with child," how Mary's hopes for her son resonated with me. She heard the angel say that He would be God's Son and exclaimed in praise, "With all my heart I glorify the Lord!" She knew He was destined for great things.

And yet it is easy to lose track of those dreams, to forget the thrill of expectation. My sons have done marvelous things, far greater than I could ever have imagined. But there were moments when I wondered if they'd even get through algebra or French or middle school or soccer or sleepaway camp. Fear can rob us of hopes and dreams.

The same thing happened to parents in the Bible. I was thumbing through the Good Book and noticed how, in the Gospel of Luke, only a few dozen verses after Mary gave birth to her firstborn, the angels' song ringing in her head, worries got the best of her.

Jesus was twelve years old and had gone with His parents to Jerusalem for Passover. Mary and Joseph were heading home when they realized He wasn't with them. They hurried back and combed Jerusalem for three days, only to discover Him, at last, sitting among the teachers at the temple. "Why have You treated us like this?" Mary asked. "Your father and I have been worried."

"Didn't you know it was necessary for me to be in my Father's house?" Jesus asked. Indeed, didn't she know? Hadn't she remembered?

Go ahead, dream great dreams for your children, commit them to prayer, give them all the love you have, and then let go. Let the Lord take our children far, leading us to places we'd never expect to go.

Let Us Pray

I turn my worries over to You, Lord, so I can be filled again with hope, not fear.

Further Reflection

LUKE 1:45 (CEB)

Happy is she who believed that the Lord would fulfill the promises he made to her.

LUKE 2:14 (CEB)

Glory to God in heaven, and on earth peace among those whom he favors.

Never Give Up Hope

MARION BOND WEST

Hope does not disappoint.

ROMANS 5:5 (NASB)

I have a homeless son.

I recently had to accept that truth. My twin sons, Jon and Jeremy, have led troubled, often dangerous, lives for decades. They have chosen not to go by the rules. Drugs, alcohol, imprisonment, and mental illnesses have plagued them.

Jon sleeps at a homeless shelter and walks to First Presbyterian Church to receive a big breakfast, sermon, and mail each Sunday. He calls me when he can borrow a friend's cell phone. Jon remains optimistic. He gets that from his father, not from me. Most of my life, I've battled fearful thoughts. I can send him a debit card in care of the church. He doesn't seem to want or need much. He assures me he loves us, but he doesn't want to see us. Not now.

He phoned one day. "It's Jon, Mom."

How could I not recognize my own son's voice? He was joyful, as usual.

"I have to have a chest X-ray. My TB test didn't come back right. I can walk to a clinic in two weeks. I'm sure it'll be fine."

I called all our family to pray and battled my negative thinking. Two weeks and four days passed. I answered the phone early one Monday, a week before Easter.

"Hey. How are you?"

"Jon?"

"Yeah, it's me, Mom. I'm good. How about you? My chest X-ray was fine. I now have to get a driver's license for twenty-five dollars."

"I'll put a gift debit card in the mail."

"Thanks, Mom. As soon as I get my license, I believe I have a job and a place to live with a buddy."

"You never give up hoping, do you, Son?"

"Of course not! You have to hang on to hope. I love you. Happy Easter!"

Let Us Pray

Father, almost everything I've learned about hope has come from my sons.

Further Reflection

JOB 13:15 (NASB)

Though He slay me, I will hope in Him. Nevertheless I will argue my ways before Him.

PSALM 39:7 (NASB)

And now, Lord, for what do I wait? My hope is in You.

One Thing at a Time

EDWARD GRINNAN

*Therefore I tell you, do not
worry about your life.*

MATTHEW 6:25 (NIV)

I woke up this morning, Monday, and all my worries were marching on me like an army. There were financial issues, work deadlines, a medical test I kept putting off, an old friend struggling with depression whom I just couldn't seem to reach out to. It was one thing after another, guilt and anxiety. Did I mention it was Monday?

I'm one of those people for whom Monday mornings are a frequent struggle. I've given up trying to figure out why. I mean, shouldn't Sundays prepare me for Mondays? Was my faith so hollow that I gave in to all of my troubles before the week had even started? *Lord,* I wanted to pray, *I'm sorry I'm such a faithless wretch.*

All at once, I remembered a craggy old voice emanating from the back room of a church basement, the voice of one of the old-timers at a twelve-step program I'd attended for years: "One thing at a time!"

That was this old guy's prevailing wisdom for just about any difficulty: *One thing at a time.* It is a popular slogan of the program, and hearing it rumble from deep within this otherwise taciturn fellow always made me smile.

Now, on this Monday morning, I needed to hear it. And I did, as clearly as if he were sitting in my living room. *One thing at a time.*

I sat on the edge of my bed and, one by one, handed each of my worries to God: finances, work, health, relationships. Every time I reached out my hand and spread my fingers wide, releasing my worries quite deliberately to a loving power greater than any trouble that could ever befall me. With each release, my mind eased, my perspective shifted, and I felt myself smile just a little, which is big for a Monday.

Let Us Pray

OK, Lord, the week can start. I'm ready now
that I've put my worries before You and
You before my worries.

Further Reflection

MATTHEW 5:36 (NIV)

And do not swear by your head, for you cannot make even one hair white or black.

LUKE 12:25–26 (NIV)

Who of you by worrying can add a single hour to your life? Since you cannot do this very little thing, why do you worry about the rest?

Expect the Unexpected

ERIN MacPHERSON

Sovereign LORD, you are God! Your covenant is trustworthy, and you have promised these good things to your servant.

2 SAMUEL 7:28 (NIV)

I t must have poured last night," I said, shaking my husband awake.

He rolled over and blinked at me sleepily. "We weren't supposed to get any rain."

"Well, there are at least 4 inches of water in our driveway."

Suddenly, Cameron was wide awake. He raced out the front door to find our front yard submerged in a giant pool of water. Our water main had broken overnight. The plumber was able to stop the deluge—for five hundred dollars.

A few days later, I noticed the light in the refrigerator was off. Seven hundred dollars and three days of eating food out of a cooler later, we learned that our main board had gone out. Next, it was the dryer; four hundred dollars and two weeks of borrowing my mom's laundry facilities. Then it was the car battery, the natural gas tank, our son needing stitches at the local urgent care facility.

By the end of the month, we were three thousand dollars in the hole and not really sure how we were going to dig our way out. I panicked, chastising myself for not saving a bigger emergency fund and my husband for not knowing how to fix things. I fretted and worried and calculated.

Trust Me, God whispered. I ignored Him in my quest to find my own answers and worried some more, allowing my anxiety to nearly suffocate me.

Two days before the bills came due, my phone rang. It was our accountant. He had made a mistake on our taxes, and we were getting an unexpected refund of $3,033. And that's when I remembered God's whisper and said my own: *Thank You, Lord!*

Let Us Pray

Lord, what an answer to prayer! No matter what outcome occurs, help me to learn to trust You. Amen.

Further Reflection

PSALM 13:5 (NIV)

But I trust in your unfailing love; my heart rejoices in your salvation.

PROVERBS 28:26 (NIV)

Those who trust in themselves are fools, but those who walk in wisdom are kept safe.

Run Free

KIM TAYLOR HENRY

Anxiety weighs down the heart.

PROVERBS 12:25 (NIV)

Whose favorite room was this? What did she say about that doorway?

I adjusted my earphone and tried to focus on the tour guide's description of the Byzantine architecture. Here I was, in the entertainment rooms of the Royal Palace of Dedinje in Belgrade, Bulgaria, yet I'd missed most of the commentary. I'd followed our group from room to room, but my thoughts were several thousand miles away.

An early morning email from one of my daughters told me of an important decision she was facing. Since then, my mind went back and forth rehashing her options. I'd planned this amazing trip for months, wanting to savor every moment, yet I was so distracted with concern I barely noticed my surroundings.

I sighed, shaking my head. Then I remembered the horses.

My daily walk at home in Colorado takes me past our neighbors' horse farm; they breed Morgans. I enjoy watching these stately animals prance and kick up their heels in their pens. But I'd noticed something curious. Every time I see two of the horses in a pasture beyond the pens, they're walking back and forth along the fence. I keep waiting for them to enjoy the expanse of several acres, but they don't. I learned that horses often pace when they're anxious. Instead of running free, they wear a track in the ground from retracing the same spot so many times.

I was doing the same thing—letting anxiety carve a rut in my mind. In that moment, I looked up at the extraordinarily beautiful expanse looming all around me and thanked God for this fantastic trip.

Let Us Pray

Lord, I turn this over to You. Lead and guide our daughter to do Your will.

Further Reflection

PSALM 37:8 (NIV)

Refrain from anger and turn from wrath; do not fret—it leads only to evil.

PSALM 68:19 (NIV)

Praise be to the Lord, to God our Savior, who daily bears our burdens.

PROVERBS 14:31 (NIV)

Whoever oppresses the poor shows contempt for their Maker, but whoever is kind to the needy honors God.

PROVERBS 21:31 (NIV)

The horse is made ready for the day of battle, but victory rests with the LORD.

God Paves the Way

SHAWNELLE ELIASEN

You hem me in behind and before,
and you lay your hand upon me.

PSALM 139:5 (NIV)

Lonny and I were driving home. We'd been to an early morning appointment, and the weather was wild. Heavy snowflakes swirled. The roads were already thick with white, and it was supposed to snow all day. I felt safe with my husband behind the wheel.

After arriving home, Lonny got ready to go to work and I gathered our younger sons and got ready to venture out.

"Are you sure you need to visit your friend today?" he asked.

"We've planned this day for weeks," I said.

"I wish you'd stay home."

"You're sweet, but it's not far."

It wasn't—just up the highway and a mile along the Mississippi River. But once in the van with my boys, I wished I'd listened to Lonny. The road had disappeared, and the choppy, brown ribbon of water was threatening and close. I moved slowly, anxiety curling my hands tight.

That's when I saw lights in my rearview mirror. Lonny had been following me; I was safe.

When I pulled into our friend's driveway, my husband pulled in, too, and tapped my window. "When you leave, call," he said. "I'll escort you home."

Lonny's chivalry reminded me of the way God has moved with us. We've had some rough roads this year, growing our teenage son. Often it has been hard to discern the path, and we've been afraid. But I can see that God has always been there for us, paving the way with His Word, protecting us from behind by sending sweet souls to support, help, and pray for us. We were hemmed in.

Lonny left, and the boys bolted to our friend's door. But I sat in silence for a moment, grateful for hemming, for safety within the seams.

Let Us Pray

When I'm afraid, Lord, help me to remember You're there. Amen.

Further Reflection

PSALM 138:7 (NIV)

Though I walk in the midst of trouble, you preserve my life. You stretch out your hand against the anger of my foes; with your right hand you save me.

1 THESSALONIANS 3:3 (NIV)

. . . so that no one would be unsettled by these trials. For you know quite well that we are destined for them.

Name Your Fears

CAROL KUYKENDALL

*For I am the L*ORD *your God who takes hold of your right hand and says to you, Do not fear; I will help you.*

ISAIAH 41:13 (NIV)

"What are you afraid of?" the emergency room doctor asked me, her face close to mine as my tears came, tears I'd tried so hard to hold back.

It was a few minutes after midnight, and I'd gone to the ER with a painful intestinal blockage, a periodic result of my ovarian cancer surgery years ago. The doctor had ordered some tests, and she'd just returned to tell my husband, daughter, and me that I was being admitted but would be taken by ambulance to the other hospital across town as soon as a bed opened up.

All I wanted to do was to go home to my own bed with my own husband.

"What are you afraid of?" she asked again, but I couldn't find words. So she continued talking about details and then left. I insisted that my husband and daughter go home, which they did. Soon I was alone with God, so I talked with Him.

What am I afraid of? Words came slowly. Being alone in the middle of a dark night, in a hospital that brings back painful memories of surgeries and facing so many unknowns.

Naming those fears in conversation with God took some of the power out of them, especially as I remembered His faithfulness within those painful memories. By 2:00 a.m., when I was wheeled into an ambulance, I felt less alone and less afraid.

Let Us Pray

Lord, I know that when I name my fears and lift them up to You, You reshape them and replace them with Your promises and peace.

Further Reflection

PSALM 46:1–3 (NIV)

God is our refuge and strength, an ever-present help in trouble. Therefore we will not fear, though the earth give way and the mountains fall into the heart of the sea, though its waters roar and foam and the mountains quake with their surging.

2 THESSALONIANS 3:16 (NIV)

Now may the Lord of peace himself give you peace at all times and in every way. The Lord be with all of you.

God Will Guide Us

EDWARD GRINNAN

Do not be afraid, nor be dismayed, for the
LORD your God is with you wherever you go.

JOSHUA 1:9 (NKJV)

In an email to one of my brainy friends, I mentioned that Macedonia might join NASA, which could cause tensions in the region. He emailed back with a laughing emoji and wrote, "Are you saying that now those pesky Macedonians are causing trouble in outer space?"

Of course, he knew I meant NATO and so did I, but little slipups that amused me in my fifties can really unnerve me in my sixties. And I am convinced that I have more to worry about than most people my age.

Alzheimer's has taken a toll in my family. My mother and both of her sisters died of it, as did their father. Now some of my older cousins on that side of the family are showing symptoms. So for me, every little slip of the tongue, every dumb auto-corrected typo, and every forgotten name spell doom.

Later, another friend, Todd, asked me, "If there were a test that could tell you if you're going to get Alzheimer's, would you take it?"

I thought for a moment and then said, "Probably not, if there wasn't anything I could do about it."

Todd smiled. "Isn't that pretty much true of the future in general? We have very little idea what will happen to us. There's not much we can do about it except live one day at a time and trust that God will guide us."

It was a lesson I should have been able to glean for myself. Trust is one of the tenets of my faith. Yet I often allow fear and anxiety to cloud my thinking and undermine my outlook. I don't always trust that a loving God has laid a path before me. I shook Todd's hand, grateful for the reminder to trust God.

Let Us Pray

Lord, I must not be fearful of the future, despite its great unknowns, for You are always there.

Further Reflection

PSALM 139:7–10 (NKJV)

Where can I go from Your Spirit? Or where can I flee from Your presence? If I ascend into heaven, You are there; if I make my bed in hell, behold, You are there. If I take the wings of the morning, and dwell in the uttermost parts of the sea, even there Your hand shall lead me, and Your right hand shall hold me.

ISAIAH 41:10 (NKJV)

Fear not, for I am with you; be not dismayed, for I am your God. I will strengthen you, yes, I will help you, I will uphold you with My righteous right hand.

ISAIAH 46:4 (NKJV)

Even to your old age, I am He, and even to gray hairs I will carry you! I have made, and I will bear; even I will carry, and will deliver you.

Use the Verses

KATIE GANSHERT

In all circumstances take up the shield of faith, with which you can extinguish all the flaming darts of the evil one; and take the helmet of salvation, and the sword of the Spirit, which is the word of God.

EPHESIANS 6:16–17 (ESV)

What was supposed to be a fun, romantic evening spiraled quickly into a nightmare. My husband and I were enjoying a date when the text came: Congolese immigration would no longer allow adopted children to leave the country. This would be effective for up to twelve months. And here we thought we'd be bringing our daughter home in just a few months!

Needless to say, my husband and I didn't finish our date. I was sick to my stomach. We hurried home to get online so we could figure out what was going on. The US Embassy in the Democratic Republic of Congo confirmed the news. It didn't take long for my mind and heart to spin into a black hole of worry and doubt.

I started emailing with two of my friends who were also adopting children from the Congo. They were spinning alongside me, until one of them offered up a Bible verse. That's all it took. Suddenly, these friends were firing off Scripture references: Exodus 14:13–14, Nahum 1:7, Matthew 10:29, Hebrews 10:22–23.

My friends were wielding the one and only, all-sufficient weapon God has given us to fight the enemy. Even though their knees were shaking and their hearts were breaking, they drew their swords, and I felt as if I could breathe again.

Let Us Pray

God, Your Word is power and truth. When the world spins out of control and worry and doubt close in, help me to bravely hold up Scripture.

Further Reflection

ZECHARIAH 4:6 (ESV)

Then he said to me, "This is the word of the Lord to Zerubbabel: Not by might, nor by power, but by my Spirit, says the Lord of hosts."

HEBREWS 4:12 (ESV)

For the word of God is living and active, sharper than any two-edged sword, piercing to the division of soul and of spirit, of joints and of marrow, and discerning the thoughts and intentions of the heart.

God Sees the Heart

ROBERTA MESSNER

For God sees not as man sees, since man looks at the outward appearance, but the LORD looks at the heart.

1 SAMUEL 16:7 (NASB)

My disfigurement was visible to most people only if I removed my eyeglasses. But still, I was devastated. When I returned to my job at the Veterans Affairs Medical Center, I stayed in my office as much as possible and brought my lunch from home.

One afternoon, I got a phone call. "I read in *Daily Guideposts* today that you have neurofibromatosis," she said, sobbing. "My daughter does too. She has a tumor on her face. We're scared."

I wanted to make certain I provided the woman with the most current information, so I looked up the disorder on the Internet. The worst pictures I'd ever seen appeared on my computer screen. One young man, a highly unusual case, had a facial tumor that hung in folds and completely engulfed his left eye.

As I answered the woman's questions, I surprised myself by ending the conversation with something my own mother always told me: "Don't forget, God sees the heart. Your little one is always beautiful in God's eyes. If you ever have any doubts, look in your Bible at 1 Samuel 16:7."

It was what *I* most needed to hear as well.

Let Us Pray

Thank You for Your reminder of true beauty, Lord.

Further Reflection

PSALM 34:5 (NASB)

They looked to Him and were radiant, and their faces will never be ashamed.

PROVERBS 31:30 (NASB)

Charm is deceitful and beauty is vain, but a woman who fears the LORD, she shall be praised.

1 PETER 3:4–6 (NASB)

. . . but it should be the hidden person of the heart, with the imperishable quality of a gentle and quiet spirit, which is precious in the sight of God. For in this way the holy women of former times, who hoped in God, also used to adorn themselves, being subject to their own husbands, just as Sarah obeyed Abraham, calling him lord; and you have proved to be her children if you do what is right without being frightened by any fear.

~ DEVOTION 35 ~

"Take Away the Disgrace"

JACQUELINE F. WHEELOCK

Take away the disgrace I dread.

PSALM 119:39 (NIV)

Last summer, I was preparing for a rare trip to visit one of my nieces when I found myself putting too much equity into what I would wear while there. I always know when the scale is tipping away from excitement toward frustration, and as I scurried around the house readying myself for the flight, I felt my anxieties skyrocketing.

"Why," I asked myself, "am I turning an event I have so looked forward to into a veritable chore?" I was reshaping a potential joy into a near-dread event, and deep down, I understood the reason: fear of facing the inevitability of aging.

I'm slower and they'll know it. I'm fatter and they'll see it.

I was dreading the reality of my loved ones seeing the person I had become.

Then I read Psalm 119, which prodded me to seek the ageless One. "Take away the disgrace," it read, which I was unwittingly allowing my golden years to become. I began to reset my priorities. I saw myself not for who I was in the flesh but for who I am in the Spirit: a blessed woman of God who has been given the gift of maturity. What the enemy of my peace, through the culture I live in, had insidiously suggested was *dis*grace was, in truth, *grace.*

Whether the psalmist suffered reproach from his own sins or from anticipation of what lie ahead from his mocking enemies, without God's grace the result was the same: dread. But through prayer and supplication, we are able to turn situational anxiety into confident peace.

Let Us Pray

Lord, thank You for access to the Holy of Holies, where dread can be turned into rest.

Further Reflection

2 CORINTHIANS 4:16 (NIV)

Therefore we do not lose heart. Though outwardly we are wasting away, yet inwardly we are being renewed day by day.

HEBREWS 4:15–16 (NIV)

For we do not have a high priest who is unable to empathize with our weaknesses, but we have one who has been tempted in every way, just as we are—yet he did not sin. Let us then approach God's throne of grace with confidence, so that we may receive mercy and find grace to help us in our time of need.

Sing a Song

PAM KIDD

I will sing.

1 CORINTHIANS 14:15 (KJV)

I'm over here," my mother calls as I walk into the hospital's big gathering room. She has been ill and is here for an evaluation.

After we exchange the usual news, her voice drops. "Oh, you just can't believe the poor woman who shares my room," she says. "Last night was awful. She kept crying on and on."

I look at my mother. Her still beautiful face is filled with compassion.

"I tried to talk to her, but she wouldn't listen. She cried like a baby. Finally, I had an idea. Maybe it would help if I sang to her."

My mother described the long night and the songs she sang. Soon the woman became quiet and peaceful and drifted off to sleep. A while later, she woke my mother, asking, "Would you please sing to me some more?"

So, through the night, my mother sang—church songs, children's songs, songs from the past.

I had come to the hospital worried. What if my mother was different, in pain, complaining, begging me to take her out of this place? But my worries were unfounded. She was the same: focused on the needs of someone else, never complaining, never talking about getting old or lamenting her loss of mobility or the fact that most of her friends had left the earth. She had become a love song.

Let Us Pray

Father, let me grow in kindness, in mercy, in love, like my mother, singing Your comfort to others.

Further Reflection

PSALM 103:2–4 (NKJV)

Bless the LORD, O my soul, and forget not all His benefits: who forgives all your iniquities, who heals all your diseases, who redeems your life from destruction, who crowns you with lovingkindness and tender mercies.

EZEKIEL 33:32 (NKJV)

Indeed you are to them as a very lovely song of one who has a pleasant voice and can play well on an instrument; for they hear your words, but they do not do them.

A Loving Friend

RICK HAMLIN

Peace I leave with you. My peace I give you. I give to you not as the world gives. Don't be troubled or afraid.

JOHN 14:27 (CEB)

I headed out to the park for my morning run. I had such a passel of worries somersaulting through my brain that I could hardly take in the sun rising behind the clouds, flushing the sky with pink, nor the daffodils opening up in brave yellow flanks on the hillside. Not for nothing did Jesus say, "Consider now the lilies."

I was on my first loop, dreading the hill, my steps slowing, my thoughts stuck on an absurd cycle of looming weariness and decrepitude, when I saw a runner in a fluorescent-green jacket coming toward me. Was that Jim? Yes, it was. A history professor and writer, he's always got something interesting to say.

"Can I join you?" he asked.

"Please," I said.

The next two loops flew by as we discussed the book he was writing, the class he was teaching, how our sons were doing, and just how much easier it was to run uphill with a companion.

"Thanks a lot," I said as we parted ways. "You were just what I needed."

"You were too," he said. "I never go that fast by myself."

"I've forgotten already what I was worrying about."

All the way home, my eyes were open to the beauty of the day. Call it endorphins, call it sunshine, but I'd say friendship was my boon companion. I recalled something preacher and writer Max Lucado once said: "When you're really down, when you're losing faith from excessive worry, get with your loving friends. They'll lead you back to God."

Two loops with my pal Jim did just that.

Let Us Pray

I give thanks, Lord, for the bounce that
friends always put in my step.

Further Reflection

PROVERBS 12:25 (CEB)

Anxiety leads to depression, but a good word encourages.

ECCLESIASTES 4:9 (CEB)

Two are better than one because they have a good return
for their hard work.

Mini the Calf

ERIKA BENTSEN

The LORD is good to all, and His tender mercies are over all His works.

PSALM 145:9 (NKJV)

On our family cattle ranch, calves usually weigh seventy to ninety pounds when they are born. But Mini started life as a vigorous, full-term, twenty-pound calf. She was so petite, it was comical. She made people smile whenever they saw her. Her sunny, friendly disposition grew as she got older, but her body never did. As the time came to wean the calves from their mothers, Mini was more than two hundred pounds lighter than her age group.

A new worry developed: *What do we do with Mini?* We couldn't keep her, but we didn't have the heart to send her to some anonymous auction yard. We ran an ad online. Every day I prayed, "Please, Lord, help us find a home for Mini." Weeks passed, and I began to lose hope that anyone would want a runt calf who would never really grow up.

I don't know why I worried. God looks after even the least of us. A family living 50 miles away called. They had young

children and a tiny farm. They wanted a small, friendly cow for their kids, but they didn't want to start a herd. It was a perfect fit. God saw to it that Mini would continue being showered with big smiles for the rest of her life.

Let Us Pray

Thank You, Lord, for giving Mini a forever home. You have shown me that the greatest charity happens when it is directed toward the least among us.

Further Reflection

PROVERBS 14:21–22 (NKJV)

He who despises his neighbor sins; but he who has mercy on the poor, happy is he. Do they not go astray who devise evil? But mercy and truth belong to those who devise good.

1 JOHN 4:16–19 (NKJV)

And we have known and believed the love that God has for us. God is love, and he who abides in love abides in God, and God in him. Love has been perfected among us in this: that we may have boldness in the day of judgment; because as He is, so are we in this world. There is no fear in love; but perfect love casts out fear, because fear involves torment. But he who fears has not been made perfect in love. We love Him because He first loved us.

The Miracle of Arguing

BRIAN DOYLE

Then Jesus said to them, "A little while longer the light is with you. Walk while you have the light, lest darkness overtake you; he who walks in darkness does not know where he is going."

JOHN 12:35 (NKJV)

Everyone talks about praying to God, appealing to God, and celebrating and praising and thanking God, but no one ever talks about arguing bitterly with God. I was arguing with the Mercy last night. I was telling Him that I am terrified for my oldest child, who has been lost in the darkness for years, and we are all exhausted dealing with her and her demons. While I love her beyond measure, she is driving me nuts, and I am furious and sad and down to my last drops of energy.

He said, *What, are you saying you want to quit? Because you begged Me for that kid, and I gave you that kid, and if you say you love her, then you are going to have to prove it every day for the rest of your life.*

I said, "Can't You cut us a break here and lift her darkness? Is that so much to ask? We are all wiped out, and I worry that the fabric of the family is fraying. I would give anything to

see a happy, healthy, cheerful woman emerge like a phoenix from the mess of the present occupant, who seems like such a stranger sometimes that I wonder if I dreamed the first happy fifteen years of her life."

He said, *All you can do is love her. Trust that there is holy joy in her and maybe somehow she will find her way there. Trust that I abide in her and she in Me. Miracles are born in love and faith.*

Well, regardless of His terse mood, I knew He was right, so I piped down and went back to plodding on and praying, trusting that God would heal us all. On we go, brothers and sisters. On we go.

Let Us Pray

Lord, I am quietly begging You here: heal my child.
Bring her back to who she is and can be.

Further Reflection

ISAIAH 58:8 (KJV)

Then shall thy light break forth as the morning, and thine health shall spring forth speedily: and thy righteousness shall go before thee; the glory of the Lord shall be thy reward.

Love from a Child

JULIE GARMON

It's a good thing to quietly hope.

LAMENTATIONS 3:26 (MSG)

God answered my secret prayer. I became a grandmother, although not in the typical way. My daughter Katie married Chris, who had a three-year-old named Rilynn. Together, they chose the most wonderful name for me: Grandma Jewels.

Rilynn already had two grandmothers. Did she have room in her heart for one more?

A few months after the wedding, Katie asked me to keep Rilynn overnight. I'd pick her up from preschool and spend the night at their house. But she barely knew me. Would she feel uneasy around me? Should I dare to let myself hope for a special relationship?

When I pulled into the preschool parking lot, excitement and fear bubbled up. *Lord, can this possibly work? We're brand-new to each other.* After signing in, I went outside to where the children were playing.

There she is. My granddaughter. Laughing with friends.

Rilynn's long blonde hair blew in the breeze. She glanced my way. Careful not to invade her space, I stood still and waved. "Grandma Jewels!" she yelled across the playground and raced toward me with her arms wide open. "You came to get me!" I bent down. She hugged me, sure and strong.

She chattered about her day, the same way Katie used to. She showed me where they kept crackers and juice boxes, and we had an afternoon snack and played dolls. Later, I went to fix supper.

"Grandma Jewels"—she tapped my leg—"could you play with me, please? For just one more minute?"

"Of course, Rilynn. I'll play with you for lots more minutes."

Let Us Pray

Father, You're full of good surprises! Help me not to be afraid to hope in every situation.

Further Reflection

PSALM 147:11 (MSG)

Those who fear GOD get GOD's attention; they can depend on his strength.

ROMANS 5:5 (MSG)

Quite the contrary—we can't round up enough containers to hold everything God generously pours into our lives through the Holy Spirit!

Leap of Faith

CAROL KUYKENDALL

So do not fear, for I am with you.

ISAIAH 41:10 (NIV)

O-ma! O-ma! O-ma!" the daunting chant grew louder, and I felt the need for bravery stirring inside me. I can do this!

Our family was spending a week on the shore of a mountain lake, and one popular activity was jumping off the end of the long dock into deeper water. Each adult and child had been dared to do it, and one by one, most had. Even the youngest, wearing her floaties, had jumped into her father's arms.

Now the whole group was daring me to jump. Truth is, my jumping days were way behind me, and I feared disappearing into that murky green water. It wasn't unsafe, just scary.

"O-ma! O-ma!"

It was now or never. This was the last day of vacation. My last chance to prove I wasn't too old to try scary things.

Though fully dressed, I willed my feet to slowly head toward the end of the dock. There was no turning back. I tried to pick up speed, praying for bravery. Just as I took my last step off the platform, I reached back and grabbed a round metal post that anchored the dock to the lake bottom below. I was struck by the shock of the cold water, the muffled sounds of water in my ears, and a jolting pain in my arm. I resurfaced to wild cheers, so I didn't acknowledge my discomfort. I merely took a shaky bow and marched off to change my clothes.

I felt that pain all night long, and more than six months later, I sometimes still felt it, a reminder that when I choose to take a leap of faith, I need to let go of fear and bravely go forward.

Let Us Pray

Lord, doing scary things reminds me that I need to trust You.

Further Reflection

PSALM 73:26 (NIV)

My flesh and my heart may fail, but God is the strength of my heart and my portion forever.

PHILIPPIANS 4:6–7 (NIV)

Do not be anxious about anything, but in every situation, by prayer and petition, with thanksgiving, present your requests to God. And the peace of God, which transcends all understanding, will guard your hearts and your minds in Christ Jesus.

Comfort in the Dark

MARION BOND WEST

*With all our tribulation and in spite of it,
[I am filled with comfort].*

2 CORINTHIANS 7:4 (AMPC)

Family and friends surrounded me while Gene was in surgery. The surgeon would repair a spiral break that involved his left hip and femur. He'd said Gene wouldn't be able to put any weight on that leg for three months. I was deeply concerned about his recovery. But I felt guilty about a ridiculous concern for myself. I didn't want anyone to know I couldn't sleep in my house alone. When darkness closes in, I become wide awake.

Gene's surgery went well, and everyone left. I sat by his bed in the semi-darkened room. He slept quietly. I grabbed my cell phone at the first hint of a ring.

"Mom," my son Jeremy said, "I want you and Gene to know I'm going to be there for you. Y'all have been there for me all these years. Even when I didn't deserve your help. I'm going to

stay with you for three months. I'll be working, but I'll spend the nights and do whatever needs doing. I'll keep the kitchen sink spotless—just the way Gene does. You just name what you need, and it will be done. You don't have to worry about anything. OK?"

"OK," I whispered and put the phone back in my purse. Jeremy had been the clown of our family and kept everyone laughing. He still does. Jeremy, who has such a passion for hard work. Dear Jeremy, who'd fought addictions and bipolar disorder fiercely, courageously. Jeremy, who'd come so near to giving up on himself but didn't. We'd be living together again after all these years. A huge measure of sweet comfort unfolded in my heart like a soft blanket.

Let Us Pray

Father, thank You for meeting each need so graciously.

Further Reflection

ISAIAH 51:12 (AMP)

I, even I, am He who comforts you. Who are you that you are afraid of man who dies and of a son of man who is made [as destructible] as grass.

1 THESSALONIANS 4:18 (AMP)

Therefore comfort and encourage one another with these words [concerning our reunion with believers who have died].

Cherry Tree Hospitality

KAREN BARBER

*Open your homes to each other
without complaining.*

1 PETER 4:9 (GNT)

Whenever I entertain, I get to worrying. *What should I cook? Will I be able to prepare it well? What if everything's not perfect?* These thoughts about the new neighbors we had invited over for dinner were going through my mind on my morning walk.

As I approached a curve in the road, I passed under a cherry tree in full bloom. I stopped to look up at the extravagant pink clusters of blossoms and recalled my girlhood days when an older couple had invited our family over with a simple yet wonderful invitation: "The weeping cherry tree in front of our house is in full bloom. We'd love for you to come over and see it." We drove up to their home and, indeed, the weeping cherry tree, as tall as their modest house, was a spectacular feast for the eyes against the deep-blue sky. They pulled up kitchen chairs because they didn't have enough seats for all of us on their small sofa and served simple refreshments: cookies from a box and sweet iced tea in ruby-red glasses. Dad took pictures of our gathering as if it were a huge celebration. What a charming, heartwarming memory!

Now I reached up and touched a cluster of soft blossoms, finding a few drops of water lingering after an overnight rain. I took the droplets and made the sign of the cross, so I wouldn't forget cherry-tree hospitality. It wasn't about perfection. It was only about welcoming others to share beautiful moments of connection and togetherness.

Let Us Pray

Dear God, help me to welcome others with the same love with which You welcome me. Amen.

Further Reflection

LUKE 10:40–42 (GNT)

Martha was upset over all the work she had to do, so she came and said, "Lord, don't you care that my sister has left me to do all the work by myself? Tell her to come and help me!" The Lord answered her, "Martha, Martha! You are worried and troubled over so many things, but just one is needed. Mary has chosen the right thing, and it will not be taken away from her."

ROMANS 12:13 (GNT)

Share your belongings with your needy fellow Christians, and open your homes to strangers.

Keeping My Eyes on the Lord

SHAWNELLE ELIASEN

*Those who pay regard to vain idols
forsake their hope of steadfast love.*

JONAH 2:8 (ESV)

I had been asked to share encouragement with a group of women from Bible study. The ladies were compassionate and kind, but still I was scared. The week before this event was an all-out battle. I was pummeled by negative thoughts. I saw myself tongue-tied, fainting and falling, breathing too fast and hyperventilating, my knees knocking together so hard the roof would fall. I recognized these as irrational, it'll-never-happen thoughts, but they hawked me just the same.

One morning, I sat in my quiet-time chair and let the fear spill like water. It was a fast rush. Worry streamed from a deep well. The bottom line was that I was afraid I'd be shamed, embarrassed, humiliated by my own ineptness. And what I understood, what was spoken to my spirit after I let the waves of worry crash free, was this: *You are making an idol—an idol of yourself, for yourself.*

This truth was both tough and tender. Suddenly, I had fresh vision and I could see the circumstance for what it was. My eyes weren't on the Lord. They were on me. Who would've thought I could build an idol this way?

I repented, and God's grace and compassion met me in a gentle, vulnerable place. So did His strength and provision, because when I talked with the women, His Spirit was there. I wasn't afraid. The words were slow and easy, and the message was strong.

Let Us Pray

Lord, keep my eyes and heart on You. Amen.

Further Reflection

ROMANS 12:19 (ESV)

Beloved, never avenge yourselves, but leave it to the wrath of God, for it is written, "Vengeance is mine, I will repay, says the Lord."

1 CORINTHIANS 10:14 (ESV)

Therefore, my beloved, flee from idolatry.

1 JOHN 5:21 (ESV)

Little children, keep yourselves from idols.

Hear His Voice

SCOTT WALKER

God saw all that he had made,
and it was very good.

GENESIS 1:31 (NIV)

I have learned that God's most natural voice is laughter and delight. When the ancient God of Genesis created the world, He bellowed across the universe, "This is good! This is very good!" God's eternal voice resounds with glee. The fruit of His labor is happiness.

Too often I have reduced God to a stern and grim voice. In my youth, I feared that God would lead me where I did not want to go. I feared that God would demand that I do what I most disliked. The God of my childhood avoided all parties and celebrations. God was warped into a demanding taskmaster.

I now know this is a distortion of sacred truth. God wants me to live in His image and share in the ongoing joy of His creativity. God longs to set me free to be my best self and to find meaningful work.

When laughter has disappeared from my life for too long and dread is the order of the day, I find that God corrects my

course and leads me in another direction. True, I have my difficult moments. But God is most intent on sharing the joy of His
creation with me—and beaming when He sees the reflection of
His image in my eyes.

Let Us Pray

Lord, to my heart bring back laughter! Amen.

Further Reflection

GENESIS 21:6 (ESV)

And Sarah said, "God has made laughter for me; everyone who hears will laugh over me."

PROVERBS 11:20 (ESV)

Those of crooked heart are an abomination to the LORD,
but those of blameless ways are his delight.

Enjoy the Precious Moments

KAREN VALENTIN

When I am afraid, I put my trust in you.

PSALM 56:3 (NIV)

Did your sister marry that man?" my father asked as we packed for a weekend at her new house. "Yes, Papi," I answered. "Remember? We went to her wedding last month."

"Ah yes, that's right, I danced with her." He shook his head and laughed, "I'm getting too old."

My father has dementia, but until that moment, I had excused his forgetfulness as being like things that would slip my own mind—where I put the hairbrush, forgetting why I walked into the kitchen, calling someone by the wrong name. That small conversation made my stomach nauseated. *It's getting worse,* I thought.

I spoke with my sister and mother about my fears, and they felt the same way.

"We have to talk about what we're going to do if it gets really bad," my sister said.

"They'll stay with me," I answered quickly. "I'm going to take care of him."

"What if you can't?" she argued. "What if it's too much for you to handle?"

"I'll get a nurse!" I said, starting to get upset. "He's never going to a nursing home."

The next few days, I could barely sleep. I'd wake up feeling sick, just thinking about my father in a nursing home.

One beautiful day, my father asked, "Do you want to go with me for a walk around the reservoir?" I was tired, but I went anyway.

We talked and laughed and even jogged a bit. It seemed he had more energy than I did. I wasn't sad or worried as we walked together. I don't know what the next few years will bring, or if he'll remember my name on his next visit to the city. But I'm not going to allow my fear of the future to steal away the precious moments we can enjoy right now.

Let Us Pray

Lord, help me to live in the moment,
not in my fears about tomorrow.

Further Reflection

LAMENTATIONS 3:21–23 (NIV)

Yet this I call to mind and therefore I have hope: Because of the LORD's great love we are not consumed, for his compassions never fail. They are new every morning; great is your faithfulness.

MATTHEW 6:27 (NIV)

Can any one of you by worrying add a single hour to your life?

Be with Her

BRIAN DOYLE

And the LORD, he it is that doth go before thee; he will be with thee, he will not fail thee, neither forsake thee: fear not, neither be dismayed.

DEUTERONOMY 31:8 (KJV)

My daughter is ill. My daughter has a condition. My daughter medicates herself—all day and night, every day, all week, all month, all year. I am her dad, and I am horrified and worried and frightened. How can this possibly end well?

My subtle, brilliant, devout, wise, gentle, gracious wife says, "Trust in God."

I said I will surely try to do so, but there I was at dusk, sobbing in the currant bushes where no one will see me losing my cool. "Fear not," You said to Isaiah, "for I am with thee." "Be not dismayed," You said, "for I am with thee." But Isaiah had no daughters, did he? He didn't lie awake at three in the morning desperate to hear the grumble of the car returning safely. He didn't try to speak reasonably and gently to his daughter and get a blast of sneer back in his face like pepper spray, did he?

How do I trust You? That is what I would like to talk about, Merciful One. Are You attending to her even as You attend to the birds of the air, who reap not? Because it sure seems to me as though she is headed for a crash, an arrest, a crisis. Do I keep playing perimeter defense and hope You are standing behind me like a huge, terrific shot-blocker? Do I accept that I cannot protect or defend her anymore? But that's an awful thing for a father to know. *You* are a Father. You know what I mean.

Suddenly, I had a flash of the oddest emotion, a terrible empathy for You, who must watch so many of Your children flail and crash. O save her, Blessed One. Please? Be with her even on her darkest paths. Please?

Let Us Pray

Dear Mercy, almost always I show up here, hat in hand, asking You to save me from myself. But today I beg desperately for my daughter. Heal her; bring her back to her deep, sweet genuine self.

Further Reflection

JEREMIAH 29:12–13 (KJV)

Then shall ye call upon me, and ye shall go and pray unto me, and I will hearken unto you. And ye shall seek me, and find me, when ye shall search for me with all your heart.

1 JOHN 5:14 (NIV)

This is the confidence we have in approaching God: that if we ask anything according to his will, he hears us.

Feeling Understood

CAROL KUYKENDALL

For when I am weak, then I am strong.

2 CORINTHIANS 12:10 (NIV)

Why did I come here today? I wondered as I slipped into my seat at the round table of our weekly Bible study. I'd just been at the doctor's office, where he'd decided to put a heart monitor on me to keep track of my increasing problems with an irregular heartbeat. My shirt did not cover up the wires and suction cups or the bulky battery at my waist, and I could feel all eyes looking at me.

These women and I were just getting to know one another. I blinked hard to hold back the tears because I did not want to talk about the heart monitor—or maybe because of my fears about tears in public. Yet they came, and someone plopped a box of tissues in front of me.

I felt totally revealed and had no choice. My words came tumbling out about feeling afraid and even a little ashamed because heart problems can come from not taking good care of yourself and not getting enough exercise or eating the wrong foods and that's not who I think I am and I don't want a heart problem and . . .

There were lots of sympathetic nods and good-listening faces and comforting words and someone praying for me. On the other side of all this compassion, I still felt a little embarrassed. But I also felt known and understood by this circle of women, my new small group. That's a good feeling.

Let Us Pray

Lord, today I learned that sharing fears—and even tears—in a safe place can be braver than trying to hide them.

Further Reflection

PSALM 34:4–5 (NIV)

I sought the Lord, and he answered me; he delivered me from all my fears. Those who look to him are radiant; their faces are never covered with shame.

1 PETER 3:8 (NIV)

Finally, all of you, be like-minded, be sympathetic, love one another, be compassionate and humble.

No Umbrellas

MARCI ALBORGHETTI

*Do not fear, for I am with you; do not be
afraid, for I am your God; I will strengthen
you; I will help you; I will uphold you with
my victorious right hand.*

ISAIAH 41:10 (NRSV)

I'm afraid of umbrellas. As a child, I'd always get my fingers
pinched trying to close them, and they never worked in the
wind anyway. Even now, especially in a sudden shower, the
button sometimes sticks or the umbrella only opens partway or
one of the metal spokes breaks.

My chronic "umbrellalessness" has earned me strange looks
over the years, not to mention comments. Most are along the
lines of "Hey, don't you know enough to come in out of the
rain?" Occasionally, people try to give me umbrellas. During a
recent downpour, a woman, whom I vaguely recognized from
church, darted out of her house with one. I was about to refuse,

but she opened it herself and stuck it in my hand, saying, "Now, dear, all of God's children deserve to stay dry!"

What an interesting thing to say, I thought. I'd been thinking a lot lately about what I deserve when it comes to God. I've never been able to fully believe that I deserve His mercy, healing, love, even grace. But I'm beginning to understand that even though I don't feel worthy, I can't forget that God's grace is the gift that He gives because I really can't be worthy.

I may still be scared of umbrellas, but I'm learning not to be so fearful of being receptive to God's grace.

Let Us Pray

Gracious God, thank You for showering Your grace and gifts upon me wherever I am, however I am. Amen.

Further Reflection

ROMANS 1:1–4 (NRSV)

Paul, a servant of Jesus Christ, called to be an apostle, set apart for the gospel of God, which he promised beforehand through his prophets in the holy scriptures, the gospel concerning his Son, who was descended from David according to the flesh and was declared to be Son of God with power according to the spirit of holiness by resurrection from the dead, Jesus Christ our Lord.

The Lord Is Good

PABLO DIAZ

I listen carefully to what God the
LORD is saying, for he speaks peace
to his faithful people.

PSALM 85:8 (NLT)

The invitation to preach at my family's gathering weighed heavily on my heart. It had been only a month since Uncle Adolfo had been diagnosed with stage four pancreatic cancer; he had a few months to live and was homebound. His daughter Elizabeth asked the family to come together for worship at her home so he could attend.

What words will bring comfort? I wondered. *What can I say to my cousins and their children that might alleviate their distress?* I was at a loss. So I did what I always do when I'm asked to preach. I prayed, "Lord, guide and help me offer words of encouragement."

Finally, after what seemed like a long wait, I felt led to Psalm 100:5 (NLT): "For the Lord is good. His unfailing love continues forever, and his faithfulness continues to each generation." The text was perfect because my uncle also taught us how to be faithful; he never wavered from God.

Although I was to give the benediction, I asked Uncle Adolfo to do it. We stood in a circle, held hands, and he gave us a blessing. It would be the last time he stood before the whole family.

Let Us Pray

Lord, thank You for Your unfailing love and faithfulness that continue forever.

Further Reflection

2 CORINTHIANS 5:7 (NLT)

For we live by believing and not by seeing.

COLOSSIANS 1:10 (NLT)

Then the way you live will always honor and please the Lord, and your lives will produce every kind of good fruit. All the while, you will grow as you learn to know God better and better.

God Is with Us— Always

JULIE GARMON

*I am always aware of the LORD's presence;
he is near, and nothing can shake me.*

PSALM 16:8 (GNT)

I attended a Christian speakers' conference, hoping God would fix my fear of public speaking. I had no idea He'd do a much deeper work.

I arrived on Wednesday and quickly bonded with the thirty-five ladies in attendance. We laughed, prayed, and worshipped together. During teaching sessions, I jotted down new topics to share. On Friday, I thought, *So far, so good. If I can just survive tomorrow.*

The next day, we'd give five-minute speeches while being videotaped.

Before the first conference began, the leaders instructed us to note comments during the presentations. As each lady spoke, my panic level rose another notch. These women would be critiquing me—and they were incredibly talented! I made the mistake of comparing myself to my new friends.

Then it was my turn. To my horror, I realized I wouldn't have time to use all my teaching aids, which were stacked beside the podium. I talked too fast and skipped important

points. Afterward, I had no idea what I'd said. Only that I'd bombed.

I texted a friend back home and explained the situation. She texted back: "Julie, focus on God. He was with you when you spoke. He's there now. He's your Redeemer. Deliverer. Savior. Counselor." I read the text. Out loud. Over and over. She was right.

Taking a deep breath, I headed back to the conference room. To my amazement, the ladies gave me an envelope full of encouraging comments. Weeks later, the link to my video arrived. Gathering my courage, I clicked it. When I watched myself speaking, I forgot about my blunders and noticed only one element: God's unfailing love shining in my eyes.

Let Us Pray

**Lord, when I remember You're with me,
nothing can shake me.**

Further Reflection

PSALM 118:6 (GNT)

The LORD is with me, I will not be afraid; what can anyone do to me?

PSALM 121:5 (GNT)

The LORD will guard you; he is by your side to protect you.

Healing through Generosity

RHODA BLECKER

*Deal loyally and compassionately
with one another.*

ZECHARIAH 7:9 (JPS)

After my husband, Keith, died, I didn't think I could give away anything of his. I was wrapping his shirts around me to replace his embrace. I wanted to keep everything because the way things were before he died was the way things were supposed to be. I couldn't bear the thought of empty racks in the closet we shared and feared I would break down. In addition to the shirts, I was also wearing his pullover fleece, his rain jacket, and his wool socks. I became determined not to part with any of his stuff, even what I couldn't wear, like his suits or his jeans.

Then someone new began posting in one of the newsgroups I frequent online. He was from Oklahoma, and he and his wife had opened their house to a homeless family. He mentioned that he played the cello and had just been accepted into a local

orchestra. "I'll have to see if I can find a tuxedo that doesn't cost too much," he wrote.

I didn't think twice before posting back: "What size do you wear? My husband's tuxedo is available, and I could send it to you for the cost of postage."

We worked out that it might fit him, and I felt not a moment's hesitation before finding the cummerbund, packaging it all up, and sending it. Alterations for the tux were minor, I'm told, but for me it was a huge change.

Let Us Pray

Thank You for making it possible for me to begin to heal, dear Lord.

Further Reflection

PSALM 112:7–9 (JPS)

He shall not be afraid of evil tidings; His heart is stedfast, trusting in the LORD. His heart is established, he shall not be afraid, Until he gaze upon his adversaries. He hath scattered abroad, he hath given to the needy; His righteousness endureth for ever; His horn shall be exalted in honour.

You Can Do It

KIM TAYLOR HENRY

For the Spirit God gave us does not make us timid, but gives us power.

2 TIMOTHY 1:7 (NIV)

To celebrate my birthday, we'll be cross-country skiing from our home to a restaurant. Hope you can join us." I stared at the email from our friends in Crested Butte, Colorado. *That sounds like fun*, I thought. I'd reached the one-year mark since my hip-replacement surgery. But skiing? *I should decline. Or maybe I can drive and meet them at the restaurant.*

I thought about my four-year-old grandson Wyatt's visit several months earlier. We were walking on our property, which contains patches of low-lying cactus. The previous day, his sister had stepped on one. Wyatt was afraid he would, too, but he didn't want to miss out on the walk, so he'd taken my hand and talked his way through the prickly areas: "You can do this. Be brave. You can do it." Once he'd done it, his smile stretched from ear to ear.

I made the decision to go.

Several weeks later, I clicked into my skis. A hefty snowfall had preceded our trek. The air was clear and frigid. Talk and laughter filled it as we joined our friends in preparation for the hour-long ski to dinner. "You can do this," I told myself. "Be brave. You can do it."

I began tentatively and then gained courage. My skis slid over crunching snow. White-robed mountains towered majestically. Brilliant stars punctuated the sky. I felt that God was with me, and my fear disappeared, replaced by exhilaration.

Let Us Pray

Thank You, God, that with You by my side, I can do it.

Further Reflection

PSALM 18:29 (NIV)

With your help I can advance against a troop; with my God I can scale a wall.

PROVERBS 3:25–26 (NIV)

Have no fear of sudden disaster or of the ruin that overtakes the wicked, for the LORD will be at your side and will keep your foot from being snared.

Do Not Fear

MELODY BONNETTE SWANG

Fear not.

ISAIAH 41:10 (NKJV)

It was a somber crowd that gathered together after the polls had closed. We were waiting to hear the results of a bond renewal election. Passage would mean additional funds to finance much-needed programs. Voting it down would mean budget cuts and layoffs. Employees were doing their best to stay upbeat, but the tension was apparent.

My boss rose to speak. In a voice heavy with emotion, he said, "I realize I have a choice. I could be a person full of fear or a person full of faith." He looked around at the crowd. "Whatever the outcome, I'm choosing to be a person full of faith. We are going to be OK, no matter what."

I was standing with coworkers, and Monica turned to me. "I sure needed to hear that," she said. "I'm waiting to hear the results of some medical tests. I want to have that kind of faith, too, but I'm just so afraid."

"I know how you feel," Sarah said. "I struggle with fear every day. I wake up with the 'what-ifs' swirling in my head! What if my husband loses his job? What if my son doesn't get his scholarship? So, every day I have to pray to *not* be afraid."

"Every day?" I asked.

"Every day," Sarah answered. She smiled. "Did you know that 'Do not fear' is written in the Bible 365 times?"

"Really?" Monica said, surprised.

"Yes," Sarah replied. "So that's a daily reminder from God to live each day without fear."

Let Us Pray

Lord, may my faith always be bigger than my fear.

Further Reflection

DEUTERONOMY 31:6 (NKJV)

Be strong and of good courage, do not fear nor be afraid of them; for the LORD your God, He is the One who goes with you. He will not leave you nor forsake you.

PSALM 27:1 (NKJV)

The LORD is my light and my salvation; whom shall I fear? The LORD is the strength of my life; of whom shall I be afraid?

On a Wing and a Prayer

PATRICIA LORENZ

One night the Lord spoke to Paul in a vision and told him, "Don't be afraid! Speak out! Don't quit! For I am with you and no one can harm you."

ACTS 18:9–10 (TLB)

During World War II, my dad was a fighter pilot in the South Pacific. His older brother, my uncle Francis, flew over the Himalayas in the China-Burma-India theater. Both of them flew hundreds of miles over uncharted terrain that encompassed rugged mountains, formidable jungles, unpredictable weather, numerous fatalities, leaky gas barrels, and exposure to enemy aircraft fire.

One time I asked Dad, "How did you survive up there in those small planes when you were under fire? Weren't you scared?"

Dad answered, "Did you ever hear the phrase 'on a wing and a prayer'? Well, it's the best way to describe how we did it. We hoped the planes would hold up long enough so we could get back to the primitive airstrips. And we prayed like our lives depended on it. That's where lifelong faith comes into play."

I've experienced fear a number of times (waiting for a diagnosis or crossing a bridge), and it always amazes me how a sincere, heartfelt prayer can calm me during scary times. It's as if the Holy Spirit soothes the trembling in my brain, allowing me to continue my journey in comfort.

Knowing how important faith was to my dad and to Uncle Francis, I now have no doubt how they both survived. Prayer saw them through, just as it sees each one of us through.

Let Us Pray

Heavenly Father, thank You for the calm that comes into my heart, mind, and soul whenever I step into a fearful place and think of You.

Further Reflection

PSALM 56:1–4 (TLB)

Lord, have mercy on me; all day long the enemy troops press in. So many are proud to fight against me; how they long to conquer me. But when I am afraid, I will put my confidence in you. Yes, I will trust the promises of God. And since I am trusting him, what can mere man do to me?

MARK 6:50–51 (TLB)

But he spoke to them at once. "It's all right," he said. "It is I! Don't be afraid." Then he climbed into the boat and the wind stopped! They just sat there, unable to take it in!

~ DEVOTION 56 ~

Abide in the Lord

SCOTT WALKER

Abide in Me, and I in you.

JOHN 15:4 (NASB1995)

Sometimes my most meaningful moments of prayer have little to do with words I speak or emotions I express to God. Rather, they have much to do with remembering and obeying a word Jesus frequently used: *abide.*

When I was a seminary student, a New Testament professor explained that the Greek word translated as *abide* means to lean back and put down your full weight on an object. It is like lying on a bed or sitting in a chair.

There are some days when I am so perplexed, frustrated, or anxious that I cannot express myself in words. I do not know how to pray. In these moments, I have a favorite reclining chair that I sit in. I prop up my feet, kick back, close my eyes, and sink into silence. I often fall asleep. In so doing, I allow myself to abide in the Lord—to put down my full weight. Often, when I awake, my life is in better perspective. I am aware that I have been in the calming presence of God.

When the apostles were crossing the Sea of Galilee and encountered a storm that threatened to sink their small boat, they grew terrified. While they were fighting the waves, Jesus was asleep at the stern. He was not overcome with fear; He was abiding in the protection of His Father.

There is a time to talk to God with words and emotion. There are other times to abide in God and simply rest in His loving presence.

Let Us Pray

Father, may I abide in Your care, knowing that You will support me through all crises. Amen.

Further Reflection

PSALM 55:22 (NASB)

Cast your burden upon the LORD and He will sustain you; He will never allow the righteous to be shaken.

MARK 4:38–40 (NASB)

And yet Jesus Himself was in the stern, asleep on the cushion; and they woke Him and said to Him, "Teacher, do You not care that we are perishing?" And He got up and rebuked the wind and said to the sea, "Hush, be still." And the wind died down and it became perfectly calm. And He said to them, "Why are you afraid? Do you still have no faith?"

1 PETER 5:7 (NASB)

. . . having cast all your anxiety on Him, because He cares about you.

No More Fright

JACQUELINE F. WHEELOCK

*For God hath not given us the spirit
of fear; but of power, and of love,
and of a sound mind.*

2 TIMOTHY 1:7 (KJV)

I'm too old for this."

My stage fright was ratcheting up. No matter that the rehearsal had gone off without a hitch, my promise to lead praise and worship service the next day had me as nervous as a first-grader summoned to the chalkboard. *What on earth made me agree to do this in the first place?* I asked myself.

I paced my bedroom floor, tested my voice. No question I loved to sing—I bombarded my husband's ears daily with songs of praise. Still, a nagging voice said, *This is organized worship. No room for an old woman's erratic creaks and squeaks.* Should I wait another month or two? Perhaps when allergy season was over, I'd have a bit more confidence.

It was too late. I had promised Doris, the praise and worship coordinator, and I had promised God.

Realizing I had forgotten to ask Doris what the theme scripture was for the next day, I trudged to my office to send a quick text message. I reached for my cell phone, and it blinked a message from the energetic young woman who faithfully plans our worship: "Forgot to tell you." I could almost hear the perpetual upbeat laugh in Doris's voice. "The theme scripture for tomorrow is 'For God has not given us the spirit of fear; but of power, and of love, and of a sound mind.'"

I smiled at the message, equivocation vanishing. I was ready to sing to the glory of God. He had spoken, and it was time to obey.

Let Us Pray

Heavenly Father, help me today to walk in Your glorious strength and not my imagined failures.

Further Reflection

PSALM 27:1 (ESV)

The Lord is my light and my salvation; whom shall I fear? The Lord is the stronghold of my life; of whom shall I be afraid?

LUKE 1:74 (NKJV)

. . . that we, being delivered from the hand of our enemies, might serve Him without fear.

1 JOHN 4:18 (ESV)

There is no fear in love, but perfect love casts out fear. For fear has to do with punishment, and whoever fears has not been perfected in love.

God's Got This

ASHLEY KAPPEL

Let us then approach God's throne of grace with confidence, so that we may receive mercy and find grace to help us in our time of need.

HEBREWS 4:16 (NIV)

I called my mom, sobbing, on the way to the hospital. "Mom," I choked out as my daughter wailed in the back seat, "Olivia broke her leg."

Two weeks before, I had stared down the barrel at a pink-eye diagnosis for my toddler, thinking about the drops I'd have to give her daily while I was thirty-nine weeks pregnant. "Lord," I prayed, "anything but pink eye. I can't handle pink eye, a toddler who touches everything, and a newborn!"

Turns out, my daughter didn't have pink eye. However, a few weeks later when my newborn was one week old, Olivia broke her leg jumping on the bed.

As I drove to the hospital, racked with emotions, my mom calmed me. "Ashley," she said, "she's breathing. Her heart is beating. All the major parts are working. If her leg is broken, we'll deal with it. Just breathe. God's got this." I took deep breaths, settling down before I arrived at the ER.

An hour later, I headed home with a sleepy toddler and a diagnosis: Olivia had indeed broken her leg. I remembered

my fear-racked prayer from weeks before. *I didn't think I could handle pink eye. How am I going to handle a newborn and a toddler in a cast?*

I couldn't. I had to depend on the help of family, friends, and, most of all, God.

Let Us Pray

God, forgive me when I put limits on Your power.
Remind me always that You are sovereign.

Further Reflection

EXODUS 23:25 (NIV)

Worship the LORD your God, and his blessing will be on your food and water. I will take away sickness from among you.

JAMES 5:15–16 (NIV)

And the prayer offered in faith will make the sick person well; the Lord will raise them up. If they have sinned, they will be forgiven. Therefore confess your sins to each other and pray for each other so that you may be healed. The prayer of a righteous person is powerful and effective.

Be Intrepid

MARILYN TURK

Jesus immediately said to them: "Take courage! It is I. Don't be afraid."

MATTHEW 14:27 (NIV)

I watched my eight-year-old grandson, Logan, race around the ice as if his life depended on it. He'd only attempted ice-skating once before, two years ago, when he hung onto the side of the rink the whole time.

Here in Florida, we don't have many places to ice-skate. After all, nothing freezes over except for an occasional puddle if we have an unusual cold snap. However, an hour west of our home is an ice arena where a hockey team plays.

For a special Scout Appreciation Day, my husband, Chuck, and I had taken Logan, a Cub Scout, to watch the hockey game. One of the event's perks was the opportunity to skate on the ice after the game was over.

Logan stepped onto the ice, testing his balance as he briefly held on to the side. Soon he was ready to fly. Never having been trained in technique didn't stop him. He ran, literally, in

circles around the ice for the next hour, skating with abandon. Of course, he had his share of falls, but they only served as temporary pauses in his pursuit before he quickly got back up and sped on.

Today's word of the day at a website I frequent is *intrepid*, meaning "resolute fearlessness, fortitude, and endurance." The example was right before me as I watched our intrepid skater.

As an adult, I am more careful and more aware of hazards and what-ifs that make me tentative about pursuing something new. Too often, I let fears hold me back. Was I ever an intrepid anything?

Jesus was an intrepid follower of God's will. Why should I fear then when He tells me not to?

Let Us Pray

Lord, when fear threatens to stop me, help me to be fearless and as intrepid as my eight-year-old grandson.

Further Reflection

JOSHUA 1:9 (NIV)

Have I not commanded you? Be strong and courageous. Do not be afraid; do not be discouraged, for the LORD your God will be with you wherever you go.

1 CORINTHIANS 16:13 (NIV)

Be on your guard; stand firm in the faith; be courageous; be strong.

Let Go of Anxiety

EDWARD GRINNAN

The LORD is my strength and my shield; my heart trusts in him, and he helps me. My heart leaps for joy, and with my song I praise him.

PSALM 28:7 (NIV)

There was a stack of them. Bills, bills, bills.

I started making payments, able to see our bank balance actually shrinking in real time online. *Can we put off this bill? Can that one wait till the next pay period? Should we just pay a partial amount on our credit card?*

Millions of Americans go through this every month. Many don't have the options my wife, Julee, and I do, even if we were short on breathing room this month. But nothing causes me greater anxiety than finances. And I know enough by now to say that the existence of great anxiety is a very reliable indicator of a lack of faith and trust.

God promised us manna from heaven. He didn't promise us cushy bank balances. In fact, Jesus seems to have frowned on excessive wealth. I detest feeling like this about money, but I dislike it more that I feel this way. Where is my trust? Where is my faith that I will be watched over and loved? Why does that faith disappear when it comes to finances even though God has always provided one way or another?

I got to the final bill. We weren't broke. We might have to cut back on a few things for a while. What I couldn't afford to cut back on, though, was my faith.

Let Us Pray

Lord, in a perverse way, I put money ahead of You when I lose sleep over bills. Yes, I have financial obligations that must be honored. But before them and all things earthly, I must honor You with my trust.

Further Reflection

2 SAMUEL 7:28 (NIV)

Sovereign LORD, you are God! Your covenant is trustworthy, and you have promised these good things to your servant.

PSALM 37:3 (NIV)

Trust in the LORD and do good; dwell in the land and enjoy safe pasture.

Just Breathe

PAM KIDD

The LORD shall give thee rest
from . . . thy fear.

ISAIAH 14:3 (KJV)

I awoke with a jolt. I was terrified. Once again, I felt as if I were being smothered. I couldn't catch my breath until I got up and walked around the house. Back in bed, apprehension consumed my thoughts.

This feeling was the result of a relatively simple problem. For some reason, my inner nose had collapsed, making it difficult to breathe properly. I'd noticed there were times when my breathing seemed a bit shallow but didn't think too much of it. Then while visiting Zimbabwe, I had a hard time while climbing the steep steps of a tower and again while dashing up a long mountain. My erratic breathing caused my heart to beat in double time, and I panicked. After I returned home, I saw my doctor. After extensive tests, he concluded that my nose was my only problem.

All I had to do was have surgery. But that's when the real fear took root. And it was made worse by comments from friends.

It's a terrible surgery. You will think you are being smothered for days. To be honest, you'll have the sensation of drowning for an entire week.

The nasal problem was getting worse, and I wasn't helping it by ramping up my anxiety level. So I called on God and centered myself there: in His presence, one moment at a time.

I was ready.

The surgery went without a hitch. Some hours later, as I began to wake up, one thing was perfectly clear. I could breathe through my nose! My doctor had cleverly inserted tubes that allowed me this forgotten pleasure. No smothering or drowning sensations. Already I could see that my problem had been solved.

How many years did I waste? How many nights' sleep did I lose? How many hours of manufactured panic did I spend separated from the one truth that waits for us all: God is with us! What shall we fear?

Let Us Pray

Father, with every breath, I breathe Your presence. I am not afraid.

Further Reflection

EXODUS 14:13 (KJV)

And Moses said unto the people, Fear ye not, stand still, and see the salvation of the LORD, which he will shew to you today: for the Egyptians whom ye have seen to day, ye shall see them again no more for ever.

MATTHEW 6:34 (KJV)

Take therefore no thought for the morrow: for the morrow shall take thought for the things of itself. Sufficient unto the day is the evil thereof.

Glimmer of Hope

KAREN BARBER

*On those living in the land of deep
darkness a light has dawned.*

ISAIAH 9:2 (NIV)

We were attending a support group to learn how best to help our son who was suffering from depression. Truth be told, I was getting depressed myself because I was finding it harder to hold on to hope as time wore on. I posed the question, "How do you help someone to see a glimmer of hope?"

One member said, "A while back, I went on a tour of the prison on Alcatraz Island. They showed us the solitary confinement cell. The tour guide said that, if we wanted, we could go into the cell and he'd close the door for a moment so we could get a feel for how dark it is in there. I went in with a few other tourists, and when he shut the door, it was totally black. I've never experienced anything like it. Then when the guide started to open the door again, even just that tiny crack of light made all the difference in the world."

The next day, I found myself trying to muster enough faith to pray for the progress I was beginning to doubt would ever happen. Then I remembered the story of the solitary confinement door being opened and how even the tiniest sliver of light penetrates the darkness. The greater it was, the less light was needed to transform it.

It was OK that I didn't have a huge amount of faith to keep on praying. All I needed was enough to pray for a small glimmer of hope.

Let Us Pray

God, I think I have enough faith today to make a difference in this darkest of times. Thank You.

Further Reflection

PSALM 112:4 (NIV)

Even in darkness light dawns for the upright, for those who are gracious and compassionate and righteous.

JOHN 1:1–5 (NIV)

In the beginning was the Word, and the Word was with God, and the Word was God. He was with God in the beginning. Through him all things were made; without him nothing was made that has been made. In him was life, and that life was the light of all mankind. The light shines in the darkness, and the darkness has not overcome it.

Holding On to Faith

MARCI ALBORGHETTI

The LORD is my strength and my might,
and he has become my salvation; this is
my God, and I will praise him.

EXODUS 15:2 (NRSV)

I had a pretty spectacular fall. Late and rushing, as always, I'd run up the two cement steps to our apartment building and, preparing to wrench open the heavy door, braced all my weight against it . . . and then missed the handle. I catapulted backward over the steps, landing on the sidewalk. Only slightly less searing than the pain was the realization that everything in my life might change because of one stupid mishap. Waiting for my husband, Charlie, and the ambulance, I felt agony, humiliation, terror.

Please, God, was all I could think, *change this! Take away this pain, this frightening helplessness!*

And now two strong women were manipulating my body for the imaging machine. With each X-ray, they grew gentler,

and I grew more afraid. One of them snatched a phone on the wall and said a few quiet, terse words: "We need more pictures."

As dread threatened to overwhelm me, the thought came that this fear and pain were just fractions of what Jesus must have felt in those hours between the Last Supper and His death. Yet He put all His trust in the Father.

Please, God, help me to do the same.

As one X-ray tech, now very careful, moved me for more images, she noticed the cross around my neck.

"Do you need to take it off?" I asked.

Her eyes met and held mine. "We're not taking that off."

Let Us Pray

**Lord, thank You for reminders of how much
I need You and need to trust You.**

Further Reflection

GENESIS 50:19–20 (NRSV)

But Joseph said to them, "Do not be afraid! Am I in the place of God? Even though you intended to do harm to me, God intended it for good, in order to preserve a numerous people, as he is doing today."

Trust Always Outshines Worry

JULIE GARMON

Let the morning bring me word of your unfailing love, for I have put my trust in you.

PSALM 143:8 (NIV)

During forty years of marriage, my husband, Rick, and I have argued about one thing in particular: I love being prepared and doing things ahead of schedule; Rick is laid-back and never worries.

One night, during the eleven o'clock news, the weatherman forecast the possibility of snow. "We better run to the grocery store," I said.

"Nah, it's not going to snow."

"What if it does? What if we lose power? The freezer's full of meat."

"Relax," he said.

"How? We could be homebound if a blizzard strikes."

Sure enough, the next morning the house was cold and dark. No power. No heat. I peered into our snow-covered backyard. "The weatherman and I were right," I said, annoyance creeping into my tone.

"I'll set up the generator," he replied, getting out of bed.

"What generator?"

"The one I bought a few years ago." Minutes later, Rick restored enough power to save the meat, keep his outdoor parakeets warm, and make coffee.

I'd doubted my husband would take care of me, the same way I'd doubted God could handle my fears and worries. Filled with admiration and gratitude, I crunched my way through our snowy yard, the air smelling woodsy, like home and wintertime and safety.

"I worried for nothing. Your survival skills are quite impressive." Rick winked at me. "Just doing my job, ma'am."

Let Us Pray

Plenty of times, I've assumed You weren't doing Your job, Lord. I'm sorry. You always have everything under control.

Further Reflection

ISAIAH 45:6–7 (NIV)

. . . so that from the rising of the sun to the place of its setting people may know there is none besides me. I am the LORD, and there is no other. I form the light and create darkness, I bring prosperity and create disaster; I, the LORD, do all these things.

JEREMIAH 29:11 (NIV)

"For I know the plans I have for you," declares the LORD, "plans to prosper you and not to harm you, plans to give you hope and a future."

Valuable Lessons

ERIKA BENTSEN

*Your word is a lamp to my feet
and a light to my path.*

PSALM 119:105 (NKJV)

I stared at the ceiling through waves of pain. Even after the
first surgery on my back had failed four years prior, the doctors were in the dark as to what was wrong. No one could fix
me. Now that I'd ruptured the disk a second time, it seemed all
I had left was God.

"Let the worst happen, Lord," I said. "I still choose You."

Something changed in the moment I surrendered everything.
It felt as though God had been waiting for me to say that.

My husband came home. "Call Nancy," he said. "She's a dairy
farmer who hurt her back just as you did, but she's already
returned to doing what she loves and it's only been seven weeks
since her surgery."

I called. Nancy not only calmed my fears, but she also made
me excited to try again. Step-by-step, she outlined what she did
to find the best surgeon in Oregon.

Doors that had long been closed began opening. This was
my miracle. The way had been laid out; I had only to follow.

The MRI showed the rupture clearly. The surgeon gave me
confidence. I was in the right place with the right doctor. I
didn't count the days until my operation; I counted the days
until my miracle.

This was God's path for me. If I had been healed before, I would have returned to life as usual and missed the faith-building lessons. I had to be broken to be restored.

Let Us Pray

You ask me to trust You, Lord, and to believe the impossible. I bury my doubts and follow You.

Further Reflection

1 SAMUEL 12:20–22 (NKJV)

Then Samuel said to the people, "Do not fear. You have done all this wickedness; yet do not turn aside from following the LORD, but serve the LORD with all your heart. And do not turn aside; for then you would go after empty things which cannot profit or deliver, for they are nothing. For the LORD will not forsake His people, for His great name's sake, because it has pleased the LORD to make you His people."

PSALM 36:9 (NKJV)

For with You is the fountain of life; in Your light we see light.

LUKE 1:37 (NKJV)

For with God nothing will be impossible.

JOHN 10:27 (NKJV)

My sheep hear My voice, and I know them, and they follow Me.

No Regrets

CAROL KUYKENDALL

He who began a good work in you will carry it on to completion until the day of Christ Jesus.

PHILIPPIANS 1:6 (NIV)

Leslie often talked about one of her greatest regrets: she was too much of a people pleaser, which made her feel self-conscious and confined one of her greatest joys, her writing.

"In school, I wrote stories and my teachers told me I was a good writer. I didn't have great confidence, but I knew I could write," she told me. "Yet my people-pleasing began to hold me back because I feared others might not like the stories. So I never shared my most creative writing, and now I regret hiding so much of myself from others."

Her description reminded me of something I've heard: the number one regret of dying people is about living a life others expected rather than living true to themselves. That was reason enough for me to try to talk Leslie out of her regrets. But the more we talked, the more I realized that I'm something of a people pleaser, too, and my talking was partly in my own defense.

"Even Jesus was a people pleaser . . . sometimes," I offered, but I'm not sure I convinced her—or myself.

I think about Jesus's last days in Jerusalem. He was not who everyone wanted Him to be, but He had the courage to always be who God created Him to be. He was a God pleaser who didn't fear what others might think. And in heaven, He redeems our regrets and unfinished business. That's a blessing for Leslie now.

As for me, it's a wake-up call.

Let Us Pray

Lord, I pray for the courage to know and to be who You made me to be on this side of heaven, and to know that You will redeem the regrets I might still be carrying when I reach the Resurrection.

Further Reflection

PSALM 139:1–6 (NIV)

You have searched me, LORD, and you know me. You know when I sit and when I rise; you perceive my thoughts from afar. You discern my going out and my lying down; you are familiar with all my ways. Before a word is on my tongue you, LORD, know it completely. You hem me in behind and before, and you lay your hand upon me. Such knowledge is too wonderful for me, too lofty for me to attain.

1 CORINTHIANS 12:18–20 (NIV)

But in fact God has placed the parts in the body, every one of them, just as he wanted them to be. If they were all one part, where would the body be? As it is, there are many parts, but one body.

One Day at a Time

SHAWNELLE ELIASEN

I consider that our present sufferings are not worth comparing with the glory that will be revealed in us.

ROMANS 8:18 (NIV)

Lonny, the three youngest boys, and I rode on the bike path that stretches alongside the river. It was finally spring. The trees held tender buds. A family of turtles sunned on driftwood. The valley was rich with endless shades of green. Everything was waking, changing. There were changes in my boys too.

Seven-year-old Isaiah steered his three-speed close to my rusty green Schwinn.

"Did you notice the difference in me, Mom?" he asked.

"What do you mean?"

"Last year, I could only make it to the bench. This year, I'm going to make it to the bridge."

He was right. Just last fall his legs gave out. He'd pushed all he could, but the bridge was too far.

"You've grown, Isaiah," I said. "You're one winter stronger."

My son smiled, pedaled, and kept his bike even with mine.

One winter stronger. I could relate.

For a long time now, a young-adult son has struggled. Watching him hurt brought deep heartache, and seeing him walk away from the things I taught him took me to a place of panic. I tried to help, but worry and fear settled strong.

Recently, though, I've begun to pray to grow in understanding—not in the circumstance but in knowledge of the Lord.

And as I one-day-at-a-time let go of fear and control and choose to claim God's powerful presence in my son's life, my faith muscles firm.

"What do you think, Mom?" Isaiah asked from under his helmet. "Race me to the dock?"

"You're on," I said. And off we went, both of us stronger.

Let Us Pray

Father, thank You for the growth that can happen during tough times. Amen.

Further Reflection

PSALM 9:9–10 (NIV)

The LORD is a refuge for the oppressed, a stronghold in times of trouble. Those who know your name trust in you, for you, LORD, have never forsaken those who seek you.

JAMES 1:2–4 (NIV)

Consider it pure joy, my brothers and sisters, whenever you face trials of many kinds, because you know that the testing of your faith produces perseverance. Let perseverance finish its work so that you may be mature and complete, not lacking anything.

1 JOHN 4:4 (NIV)

You, dear children, are from God and have overcome them, because the one who is in you is greater than the one who is in the world.

Be Fearless

KAREN VALENTIN

"For I know the plans I have for you,"
declares the LORD, "plans to prosper you
and not to harm you, plans to give you
hope and a future."

JEREMIAH 29:11 (NIV)

I posted a video of my son doing a front flip at a small open gym near my home.

"You should put him in gymnastics over here," my friend and former coworker said when he saw the video.

He still worked at the elite gym where I coached gymnastics for years before my kids were born. I had dreamed of sending my boys there. But my answer was the reason that had kept me away thus far.

"I could never afford that place," I said, wishing I could.

He encouraged me to apply for a scholarship and in the meantime send the boys in to be tested for Pre-Team. I did it.

The boys made the Pre-Team, but I had to pay full price until the scholarship committee gave me an answer. I didn't have the heart to pull them out, but I barely had the funds to keep them in. And what if I didn't get the scholarship?

I watched from the mezzanine as the boys listened to their coaches and excitedly displayed their strength and agility.

"Help me, Lord," I prayed. "If you want them here, help me find a way."

I started a GoFundMe page for my little athletes. Friends and family responded and covered three months of classes, and the scholarship committee came back with a decision to grant us 50 percent off the tuition for six months.

The boys have been training for five months and are already being moved up to the competitive team. They are fearless! And I'm learning how to be fearless right along with them.

Let Us Pray

Lord, remind me that You are the maker of my future and the provider of all I have.

Further Reflection

ISAIAH 41:10 (NIV)

So do not fear, for I am with you; do not be dismayed, for I am your God. I will strengthen you and help you; I will uphold you with my righteous right hand.

A Lesson from Snakes

SABRA CIANCANELLI

*Trust in the LORD with all your heart and
lean not on your own understanding.*

PROVERBS 3:5 (NIV)

Bent over the soil, I cleared off leaves and began to wake up
my garden by sweeping away winter's mess. My thoughts
turned to an upcoming business trip. I had volunteered for
the project and was looking forward to it, but now as it grew
near, all my excitement turned to dread. Would the flight be
delayed? Would my presentation go over well? In a flash, a
garter snake slithered right in front of my knees! My heart
jumped, and I let out a squeal.

I caught my breath, and my mind traveled back to elemen-
tary school. In fourth grade, we had garter snakes in the classroom. The first day of school, the teacher picked one up out of
the tank and strolled the aisles between our desks. The snake
slinked up his left arm, and kids backed up their chairs.

"We're afraid of things we don't understand," he said. "I'm
going to teach you all about these amazing creatures. You don't
have to touch them or go near them if you don't want to. But
I'll bet by Thanksgiving each one of you will have held one.
Anyone want to touch one now?"

I folded my arms and shook my head. I wasn't about to
touch a snake, let alone hold one.

It started out simply. For a few minutes in the morning, our teacher would go to the tank and pick one up. He showed us how snakes weren't slimy but strong. He offered facts and asked us to look closely so we could see the beauty of their scales.

It didn't even take until Thanksgiving. Before the end of September, there wasn't one of us who hadn't grown to care for what we once feared. My business trip was going to be just fine.

Let Us Pray

Heavenly Father, when worry enters my heart, help me remember that what is beyond my understanding is in Your hands. I have nothing to fear.

Further Reflection

JOHN 14:27 (NIV)

Peace I leave with you; my peace I give you. I do not give to you as the world gives. Do not let your hearts be troubled and do not be afraid.

PHILIPPIANS 4:6–7 (NIV)

Do not be anxious about anything, but in every situation, by prayer and petition, with thanksgiving, present your requests to God. And the peace of God, which transcends all understanding, will guard your hearts and your minds in Christ Jesus.

2 THESSALONIANS 3:16 (NIV)

Now may the Lord of peace himself give you peace at all times and in every way. The Lord be with all of you.

Stay Afloat

ASHLEY KAPPEL

The LORD himself goes before you and will be with you; he will never leave you nor forsake you. Do not be afraid; do not be discouraged.

DEUTERONOMY 31:8 (NIV)

Saturday afternoons at the local pool are a particular kind of crazy. Every neighborhood kid over thirteen is here alone, being cool at the snack bar and diving off the high board. Young families abound, burning the hours between naptime and dinner.

Often I brave the bedlam by myself with the kids, Brian coming to meet us later. That means I've got a little guy, only six months old, who needs me to hold him (and hates to be splashed), and two-year-old Olivia, who moves so quickly she often produces her own wake.

It doesn't take long for Olivia to get a decent distance from me, and thanks to her swimmies, I don't worry. As long as I can see her, I know she's OK.

But Olivia doesn't know that. One afternoon, it hit her that I wasn't right beside her anymore. From her vantage point, she was completely surrounded by torsos and floats and yet all alone.

I could see the panic spreading across her face as she grew more tearful and fearful by the minute. Though I was just a few feet away, to Olivia I might as well have packed my bags and headed home. I called out to her, but in her fear, she couldn't hear me. "I'm here! Just look at me! Find my face!" I called as I moved toward her.

But I know something Olivia doesn't. I can see the bigger picture. I know her mommy is there, that she is safe, that her swimmies are keeping her afloat, that she's about 4 feet from a lifeguard. All Olivia knows is that she is alone, scared, and lost.

How often do I find myself lost, alone, and adrift? How often is God just inches away, whispering, "I'm here. Just look to Me. Find My face"?

Let Us Pray

Lord, help me always to see Your face.

Further Reflection

DEUTERONOMY 31:6 (NIV)

Be strong and courageous. Do not be afraid or terrified because of them, for the Lord your God goes with you; he will never leave you nor forsake you.

PSALM 34:17–18 (NIV)

The righteous cry out, and the Lord hears them; he delivers them from all their troubles. The Lord is close to the brokenhearted and saves those who are crushed in spirit.

Mistakes Happen

JON SWEENEY

You are precious in my sight and
honored and I love you. . . . Do not fear,
for I am with you.

ISAIAH 43:4–5 (NRSV)

The problem was not that one of the boys was bigger than the others or that he was swinging too high; the problem was that the swing set simply wasn't designed to hold five kids at once.

I have nightmares about these things. I'm one of those parents who imagines the worst. And when my wife or anyone else tells me not to worry or quotes the Bible telling me why I shouldn't worry, I feel like saying, "And how exactly do I do that?"

My son and four of his friends were playing outside, and I wasn't paying close enough attention. They were enjoying themselves, and everyone seemed to be getting along. But then the swing set quite literally tipped over.

Thank God—and I mean, I thank God—the kids were all OK.

You see, despite my worrying, bad things happen. I've learned that despite my worrying, God protects my kids. I have no doubt that God wants me to keep a watchful eye on them, and I have no doubt that God would be pleased if I trusted

Him more than I do. But I also know that God cares for me and for them all the time, even though they make mistakes and I lack faith.

Let Us Pray

Thank You, God, for Your watchful eye and Your guiding hand today. I am so very thankful for both!

Further Reflection

COLOSSIANS 3:15–16 (NRSV)

And let the peace of Christ rule in your hearts, to which indeed you were called in the one body. And be thankful. Let the word of Christ dwell in you richly; teach and admonish one another in all wisdom; and with gratitude in your hearts sing psalms, hymns, and spiritual songs to God.

God Isn't Finished

BILL GIOVANNETTI

*I don't mean to say that I have already
achieved these things or that I have
already reached perfection. But I press
on to possess that perfection for which
Christ Jesus first possessed me.*

PHILIPPIANS 3:12 (NLT)

Bill! Bill! Bill!" The little company of happy people chanted
my name. They were cheering for me to cross a rickety
footbridge strung over a deep canyon.

I detest heights. So when my teenage kids asked to go
zip-lining, I planned to send them off at the beginning and
pick them up at the end.

"No, sir," I was told. "They need an adult with them."

I reluctantly volunteered. They strapped me into the harness, drove us higher than I thought safe, and walked our group
to a tiny wire and platform. When it was my turn, I bravely
stepped up and zipped. To my surprise, I had fun. "Not too
bad," I said. My kids were proud.

After the third zip, we came to the suspension bridge. It
seemed designed to provoke panic. I started, stopped, backed
up, and let others cross before me. Finally, I was the last one.

Now they all watched me, chanting my name for encouragement. My heart pounded like a rabbit's. I tried three times.

Each time I froze up. Eventually, I told them I'd just walk to the next zip line and meet them there.

When we all got together, my son asked, "Dad, were you afraid?"

I thought for a moment and said, "Son, the number one fear in this country is public speaking. I do that several times every weekend, even though it scares me. So, yes, I have some fears. Some I've conquered; some I haven't. It just means God isn't finished with me yet."

Let Us Pray

Lord, I haven't reached perfection. But please keep me going in the right direction to experience more and more of Your grace. Amen.

Further Reflection

HEBREWS 12:1–2 (NLT)

Therefore, since we are surrounded by such a huge crowd of witnesses to the life of faith, let us strip off every weight that slows us down, especially the sin that so easily trips us up. And let us run with endurance the race God has set before us. We do this by keeping our eyes on Jesus, the champion who initiates and perfects our faith. Because of the joy awaiting him, he endured the cross, disregarding its shame. Now he is seated in the place of honor beside God's throne.

Don't Forget Him

PAM KIDD

He telleth the number of the stars;
he calleth them all by their names.

PSALM 147:4 (KJV)

Sometimes I feel as if I've been forgotten. I wake up during the night and wonder, *How can I keep doing all the things I have to do? There's Zimbabwe: we take on more children every year to feed, clothe, educate. What if our resources dry up?*

And there's the community group I organize—speakers and meeting places every month. I don't want to let anyone down but . . .

And my family and friends who need me—I don't have enough time.

And on it goes. Finally, I pull myself out of bed and walk around the house.

I'm pedaling as fast as I can, God. Will I ever get to a stretch of easy going, where I can coast?

Still not ready for sleep, I wander out to the porch. A train passes in the distance. A slight breeze rustles the trees, and beyond their branches I see a slice of moon, a scattering of stars.

The darkness is calming. I reach past the worry and breathe deeply. In the stillness, something greater than myself and all my fears waits. I recall the times I've let go and trusted God. I remember how solutions beyond my understanding seemingly come out of nowhere.

The sky above is infinite, and if God's Word is true, He has every single one of those stars named. In ways I can't understand, He sees everything—even me, as I sit in the night. God will never forget me. My problem is this: sometimes I forget Him.

Let Us Pray

Father, save me from my worries. I know that if You stay close, I can coast.

Further Reflection

JOB 28:27–28 (NKJV)

Then He saw wisdom and declared it; He prepared it, indeed, He searched it out. And to man He said, "Behold, the fear of the Lord, that is wisdom, and to depart from evil is understanding."

We'll Be Fine

JIM HINCH

*God is our refuge and strength,
a very present help in trouble. Therefore
we will not fear, though the earth should
change, though the mountains shake
in the heart of the sea.*

PSALM 46:1–2 (NRSV)

It's Frances's first time at sleepaway camp. The drive is beautiful. The kids work out their nervous tension playing silly games in the back seat. Kate and I sit quietly with our mixed feelings.

Frances is nine. She has become a poised, mature, independent girl. We know she'll do fine, though we can tell she's masking her nervousness. I wonder if Kate and I are more nervous, not so much that she'll get homesick or fail to make friends, but that life is changing. The past, when the kids were little and depended on us for everything, is ebbing away. Next year, Benji will be seven, old enough to attend camp too.

Our lives have revolved around the kids for so long. Now we have to let them grow up, explore things on their own, and encourage them to become their own independent selves.

We arrive at the camp. Frances gathers with a group of kids heading to the lake for a swim. She hugs us several times, then gamely trudges off. She turns to wave, and we can see anxiousness in her smile.

Well, at least she's not glad to see us go! She, too, understands this is a big moment, a venture into the unknown.

Then I remember what we loved about this camp when we visited. They held a prayer service for visiting families in the woodsy outdoor chapel.

We'll all be fine. God is here, holding us through every change.

Let Us Pray

Lord, we change, but You don't.
Help me to remember that.

Further Reflection

NUMBERS 23:19 (NRSV)

God is not a human being, that he should lie, or a mortal, that he should change his mind. Has he promised, and will he not do it? Has he spoken, and will he not fulfill it?

MALACHI 3:6 (NRSV)

For I the LORD do not change; therefore you, O children of Jacob, have not perished.

HEBREWS 13:8 (NRSV)

Jesus Christ is the same yesterday and today and forever.

A Warm Hug

SHAWNELLE ELIASEN

Look to the LORD and his strength;
seek his face always.

PSALM 105:4 (NIV)

I lay awake. The dream had pulled me from sleep. In my slumber, my teenage son was a little boy again. His eyes were a shining blue. His smile held a lineup of baby teeth. And he laughed. It had been so long since I'd heard that sweet sound.

The past months had been tough. His father and I were weary from wading through deep waters of teen turbulence. We laid boundaries in a foundation of love, but the boundaries left us on one side of a chasm, our son on the other. The longing for a restored relationship was a physical ache in my chest.

I tossed and turned, wrestling with fears that came close in the night. I didn't want to wake my husband, Lonny. He hadn't been sleeping well either. I swung my legs over the side of the bed and hoped the sofa would offer rest, but the living room was void and vast. Our grandfather clock ticked into the emptiness. Emotion, thick as the dark, filled me. I moved to the rug, sat in the center, curled my arms over my knees, and cried.

"What are you doing?" came a voice from the darkness. In a moment, Lonny was close, his breath warm on my neck. His arms wrapped around mine, and he cradled me tight. "When you're hurting," he whispered, "please stay beside me. Don't leave. You don't have to hurt alone."

We sat for a long while in the shadow of night, in the center of our worn wool rug. As Lonny held me, I began to feel God's arms wrap around me, too, and was reminded of an even greater truth: the Lord was always with me. I didn't have to hurt alone.

Let Us Pray

Lord, thank You for holding me. Amen.

Learn What to Say

LOGAN ELIASEN

The LORD said to him, "Who gave human beings their mouths? Who makes them deaf or mute? Who gives them sight or makes them blind? Is it not I, the LORD? Now go; I will help you speak and will teach you what to say."

EXODUS 4:11–12 (NIV)

It's my first semester of law school. The lecture hall is stifling because of the seventy students crammed into it. I lean over my casebook, highlighter cap between my teeth, and I strike the text with neon blue.

"Let's take a look at the dissent," the professor says. "Why don't you walk us through the argument, Mr. Eliasen?"

The cap falls from my mouth. My face burns. It's not that I'm unprepared. I read the case three times last night. But I'm a quiet person, and seventy sets of eyes are on me now.

I'm humble; it's one of my better qualities. But sometimes our greatest strengths don't dwell far from our deepest weaknesses. My humility borders a place where feelings of inadequacy lurk and I can sense those thoughts in the back of my mind: *You're too quiet. You don't have anything worth saying. You're not a speaker.*

Then I think of Moses. The man who stood before the fiery presence of God and explained that he was too terrified to speak to a human king.

"I will teach you what to say," promised God.

I flip the pages of my casebook and then clear my throat. I'm ready to reject my fear of inadequacy. I'm ready to claim God's promise.

Let Us Pray

**Father, I'm so grateful that I can trust You
to fill my mouth with words.**

Further Reflection

JEREMIAH 1:6–8 (NIV)

"Alas, Sovereign LORD," I said, "I do not know how to speak; I am too young." But the LORD said to me, "Do not say, 'I am too young.' You must go to everyone I send you to and say whatever I command you. Do not be afraid of them, for I am with you and will rescue you," declares the LORD.

LUKE 12:11–12 (NIV)

When you are brought before synagogues, rulers and authorities, do not worry about how you will defend yourselves or what you will say, for the Holy Spirit will teach you at that time what you should say.

Spider!

RHODA BLECKER

Do not fear them, for it is the Lord your God who will battle for you.

DEUTERONOMY 3:22 (JPS)

I am uneasy about things with more than four legs, so I have always run away when confronted by spiders. I know they serve a purpose in the great scheme of things, but I'm much more comfortable when they're serving that purpose in a place I'm not. My husband, Keith, understood. All I had to do was yell, "Spider!" and he would come to my rescue.

After Keith died, I learned to do a lot of things that he used to take care of: trim the blackberry bushes, change light-bulbs in the cathedral ceiling, clean snow off the satellite dish, trap mice. These tasks were easy compared to the first time a spider challenged me. (Throwing things at spiders is not very effective.)

If I could not conquer my fear of spiders, I knew I would always be afraid they would crawl over me at night. And some

of our spiders were big enough that even the cat didn't want to have anything to do with them.

I had to make myself get close enough to them to squash them. I still yelled, "Spider!" but now it was a prayer, not a condemnation. I was learning that the only way to conquer the fear was to understand I still had support when I was scared, even if it was invisible, and even if I had to do the active rescuing myself.

Let Us Pray

Lord, thank You for being there when I face my fears because I never have been able to do that without Your encouragement.

Further Reflection

2 KINGS 6:16 (JPS)

And he answered: "Fear not: for they that are with us are more than they that are with them."

PSALM 118:11–12 (JPS)

They compass me about, yea, they compass me about; Verily, in the name of the Lord I will cut them off. They compass me about like bees; They are quenched as the fire of thorns; Verily, in the name of the Lord I will cut them off.

Good Shadows

JACQUELINE F. WHEELOCK

*He that dwelleth in the secret place
of the most High shall abide under
the shadow of the Almighty.*

PSALM 91:1 (KJV)

My oncologist walked into the examining room, devoid of her usual, "You're fine." For twenty years, she had spoken those soothing words during each of my annual visits, except two. And both of those times were painfully etched into my memory.

Handed a brush by the enemy of my soul, I had already painted a dark picture before the doctor entered. *This is the very same room you were in when you got that last "bad diagnosis,"* I reminded myself. So when the doctor said there was a shadow on my X-ray, I leaned my head back onto the chair in resignation, quickly connecting the test results with the proverbial shadow of death.

Here we go again, I thought, my insides threatening to fold.

Settling down a bit, I remembered my commitment to memorizing Psalm 91 a couple of years earlier. Thankfully, the very first verse called to mind another kind of shadow, one that comforts, protects, and guides. Three days and two sleepless nights later, after undergoing a more sophisticated scan, I found those words from the Psalms—"He that dwelleth in the secret place of the most High shall abide under the shadow of the Almighty"—taking on new meaning.

"Nothing's there. It was just a shadow," said the accompanying nurse. My calculations had been flawed. I basked beneath the protection of the life-sustaining "shadow" that is always over me. God had given me another chance to reduce my fears and realign my thinking with His precious Word.

Let Us Pray

Lord, help me to trust You past my own meager ability to reason.

Further Reflection

PSALM 121:5–8 (KJV)

The Lord is thy keeper: the Lord is thy shade upon thy right hand. The sun shall not smite thee by day, nor the moon by night. The Lord shall preserve thee from all evil: he shall preserve thy soul. The Lord shall preserve thy going out and thy coming in from this time forth, and even for evermore.

Leaving a Legacy

ROBERTA MESSNER

Therefore encourage one another
with these words.

1 THESSALONIANS 4:18 (NIV)

When my former coworker spoke the words "who I used to be," I froze in my chair. Part of the reason I feared retirement was Dad. When my father left the railroad, losing his identity was so difficult for him, he actually became suicidal.

As the days wore on and I completed work projects, I called on the heavens. "Help me to know that what I've done in my job has really meant something," I prayed. I dreaded saying goodbye to my veteran patients and their dear ones. But I also longed to leave a legacy.

One afternoon at work, our new medical center director, Mr. Nimmo, stopped by. "I'm learning you have quite a reputation, Roberta," he said. "It goes beyond your role in infection prevention. Rumor has it, whenever you teach a class, you always tell great stories about your experiences with veterans."

I smiled. My motto was always this: "When in doubt, tell a story." I'd found it was the shortest distance between two hearts.

In the nearly forty years I worked with veterans and their families, I cared for soldiers of the Spanish-American War,

World Wars I and II, the wars in Korea and Vietnam, and more recent conflicts.

Mr. Nimmo continued, "I'd love for you to help me collect a book of veteran stories, Roberta."

Before our conversation ended, I told him of my plans to retire. I also promised to stay on a little longer to help compile those stories.

Let Us Pray

Lead me to the stories You want told, Lord.

Further Reflection

HEBREWS 10:24–25 (NIV)

And let us consider how we may spur one another on toward love and good deeds, not giving up meeting together, as some are in the habit of doing, but encouraging one another—and all the more as you see the Day approaching.

HEBREWS 13:16 (NIV)

And do not forget to do good and to share with others, for with such sacrifices God is pleased.

Getting Back on My Bike

PATRICIA LORENZ

Be strong and take heart,
all you who hope in the LORD.

PSALM 31:24 (NIV)

I heard a woman on *Wheel of Fortune* say one of her dreams was to run with the bulls in Spain. I thought she was crazy. I made a list and posted it on Facebook. "Things I Will Never Do: wear false eyelashes, run with the bulls, skydive, smoke anything, get a tattoo or a face-lift. Everything else is up for grabs, especially after regaining my courage and getting back on my bicycle today."

I'd taken my first bike ride in ten months. The last time I'd tried to ride, the pain in my knees was so bad I had to get off and put the bike away after two blocks. The next month, I had both knees replaced. Double knee replacement surgery is extreme, the recuperation long and difficult. After eight months, a bad pain in the back of my right knee still kept me from bending it more than ninety degrees. But after hearing that woman say she wanted to run with the bulls, I decided it was time to get back on my bike and hope for the best.

The first few times I pushed down on the pedals, it was scary. My back tensed up. My hands clenched the handlebars. The bike wobbled. I winced in pain every time my right knee had to push down. I was terrified I would fall down when it was time to get off the bike. But I kept going. And going. Around the block. Around the block again. I went farther, around two square blocks this time. The pain behind my right knee lessened. I practically shouted prayers of thanksgiving. I rode for 2½ miles before stopping. The next day, I did 2½ miles again. Day three, almost 5 miles. Every day more miles.

Let Us Pray

Lord, when I'm fearful of scary or uncomfortable endeavors, give me courage to do them anyway. Thank You for the push.

Further Reflection

JOB 14:7–12 (NIV)

At least there is hope for a tree: If it is cut down, it will sprout again, and its new shoots will not fail. Its roots may grow old in the ground and its stump die in the soil, yet at the scent of water it will bud and put forth shoots like a plant. But a man dies and is laid low; he breathes his last and is no more. As the water of a lake dries up or a riverbed becomes parched and dry, so he lies down and does not rise; till the heavens are no more, people will not awake or be roused from their sleep.

The First Leap

ERIN MacPHERSON

Behold, I am doing a new thing;
now it springs forth, do you not
perceive it? I will make a way in the
wilderness and rivers in the desert.

ISAIAH 43:19 (ESV)

We took our puppy, Zeke, to the beach for spring break. He loved the sand, the freedom to run free, and the wind blowing his tennis ball much farther than it does in our yard at home.

But the water? He wasn't about to go in. Instead, he stood at the edge of the waves, whining at the great expanse of ocean, jumping backward each time an unruly wave came close to his feet.

Day two dawned, then day three and day four, and still Zeke hadn't touched the water.

Then, on day five, a seagull swooped down right in front of him, causing him to forget his fear for just a moment. He dived after it and splashed down on his side in the churning water.

He appeared dazed for a minute. He looked back at me, and I said, "It's OK, Zekey-boy. Go on in!"

And so he did.

He dived headfirst into the deeper water, jumped over the waves, and swam. It was a messy doggy-paddle at first as he tested out his skills, but minutes later he was smooth and sleek in the water, swimming fast enough to catch up to my kids, who played in the surf.

Of course, he loved it.

On day six, Zeke sprinted down the beach and into the surf.

When we got back home, he ran from the car and jumped straight into our swimming pool.

What had been a huge fear was now his greatest joy. He just had to find the courage to dive in and see if he could float.

Let Us Pray

Heavenly Father, give me the courage to push beyond my fears and dive headfirst into the promises You have for my life. Amen.

Further Reflection

ISAIAH 42:10 (ESV)

Sing to the LORD a new song, his praise from the end of the earth, you who go down to the sea, and all that fills it, the coastlands and their inhabitants.

EZEKIEL 36:26–27 (ESV)

And I will give you a new heart, and a new spirit I will put within you. And I will remove the heart of stone from your flesh and give you a heart of flesh. And I will put my Spirit within you, and cause you to walk in my statutes and be careful to obey my rules.

The Safety of Paths

KIM TAYLOR HENRY

You make known to me the path of life.

PSALM 16:11 (NIV)

I love to walk the fields around our home, but the grasses covering them had grown thick and knee-high. While we don't have lots of snakes on our land, I'm still wary when I can't see where I'm walking. It wasn't quite time for our annual mowing, so my treks into the pastures dwindled, then disappeared, until my husband, David, surprised me by mowing tractor-wide paths through the dense grasses. I could now walk without fear, so I followed the paths, delighting in the purple, orange, and yellow wildflowers along the way. A red-winged blackbird perched on a fence post. From a thicket, two deer leaped and bounded away. Several red-tailed hawks soared overhead.

Enjoying these mowed trails reminded me of when I was young and my father mowed paths through tall grass in our backyard. I pretended they were rooms and hallways of a big house. I felt happy and secure playing inside those boundaries.

Paths make me feel safer. They tell me that this is the way that's best. They help me circumvent dangers I might otherwise stumble upon. When hiking, I prefer to take prepared trails rather than create my own, which could lead to perils I'd rather avoid. Paths lead me to my destination. Without them, I can be fearful or get lost.

David and my father aren't my only path makers. I have a loving shepherd who leads me in paths of righteousness for His name's sake. I will fear no evil.

Let Us Pray

Thank You, Lord, for preparing the way and pointing me to it.

Further Reflection

PSALM 23:3 (NIV)

He refreshes my soul. He guides me along the right paths for his name's sake.

PSALM 25:4–5 (NIV)

Show me your ways, LORD, teach me your paths. Guide me in your truth and teach me, for you are God my Savior, and my hope is in you all day long.

ISAIAH 30:21 (NIV)

Whether you turn to the right or to the left, your ears will hear a voice behind you, saying, "This is the way; walk in it."

Stinking Thinking

SCOTT WALKER

*Can any one of you by worrying add
a single hour to your life?*

MATTHEW 6:27 (NIV)

On occasion I become fixated on a problem, fear, or issue and can't release that thought or emotion. Such fixation only distorts my perspective and weakens my health.

Today as my wife and I were vacationing at the beach, I woke up worried about our golden retrievers we left at home (with a house sitter). I also had a nagging headache. Two hours later, I'd made the headache worse by stressing about the pain, and I had certainly not helped my uneasiness about my dogs.

One of my counseling professors, Dr. Wayne Oates, called such unproductive worrying "stinking thinking." And that is right! Much anxiety is counterproductive and unhealthy, not helpful. To be blunt, "It stinks!" Why stay around the stench of our obsessive-compulsive worries?

During my prayer time, I often talk to God about my anxieties. I ask Him to help me let go of fear, prioritize what really deserves attention, and avoid "stinking thinking." It is amazing how prayer helps me do this. Soon, God's Spirit usually places another person's needs before me that are more important. Then I am free to move beyond my problems and help God actually address the needs of others.

To overcome "stinking thinking" takes more than our strength and willpower. It requires asking God to give us the "mind of Christ" and calming presence of the Holy Spirit.

Let Us Pray

Father, I lift my needs and fears to You today. Help me release them to Your care.

Further Reflection

PROVERBS 3:5–6 (NIV)

Trust in the LORD with all your heart and lean not on your own understanding; in all your ways submit to him, and he will make your paths straight.

MATTHEW 6:25–27 (NIV)

Therefore I tell you, do not worry about your life, what you will eat or drink; or about your body, what you will wear. Is not life more than food, and the body more than clothes? Look at the birds of the air; they do not sow or reap or store away in barns, and yet your heavenly Father feeds them. Are you not much more valuable than they? Can any one of you by worrying add a single hour to your life?

PHILIPPIANS 4:6–7 (NIV)

Do not be anxious about anything, but in every situation, by prayer and petition, with thanksgiving, present your requests to God. And the peace of God, which transcends all understanding, will guard your hearts and your minds in Christ Jesus.

Let's Pray!

JIM HINCH

His way is in whirlwind and storm,
and the clouds are the dust of his feet.

NAHUM 1:3 (NRSV)

I'm sure it won't rain."

Kate and I gazed above the peaks: a little cloudy but nothing unusual for early evening in the Sierra Nevadas. We were backpacking with the kids, camping at a high-altitude lake, to experience God in the wilderness.

The clouds thickened. A few raindrops speckled the granite around our campsite. "Frances, Benjamin, come closer to the tents!" Kate called. The kids jogged back from the lake, where they'd been playing.

The rain grew steadier. "OK, everyone inside," I said. Frances and Kate ducked into one tent. Benjamin and I crawled into the other.

Suddenly, our voices were drowned out. Thunder boomed and rolled. Rain poured onto the tent. The rainfly sagged. A few drips plopped onto our sleeping bags.

"Daddy!" cried Benjamin. I drew him close. The rain turned to hail. Wind shook the tent. I didn't voice my fear: that the hail might puncture the fabric, that the tent might collapse. The Sierras in summer are usually placid—until they're not. It can snow heavily at high altitude in August. Gale-force winds can snap tent poles like matchsticks.

The hail crescendoed to a roar. "Let's pray!" I shouted. In as calm a voice as I could muster, I prayed for the storm to end, for God to keep us safe.

At last, the hail slackened and turned to rain. The rain slowed to a drizzle and stopped. I let go of Benjamin, and we unzipped the tent and peered out at the clearing sky. Kate and Frances were peering out too. We grinned at one another, relieved but also awed by the storm's sudden fury.

God in the wilderness. We'd experienced Him, all right: His power, His mercy, and the power of His mercy.

Let Us Pray

Your power will be sufficient for me today, Lord.

Further Reflection

EXODUS 15:1–3 (NRSV)

I will sing to the LORD, for he has triumphed gloriously; horse and rider he has thrown into the sea. The LORD is my strength and my might, and he has become my salvation; this is my God, and I will praise him, my father's God, and I will exalt him. The LORD is a warrior; the LORD is his name.

Empathy Amid the Trains

ASHLEY KAPPEL

Jesus said, "Let the little children come to me and do not hinder them, for to such belongs the kingdom of heaven."

MATTHEW 19:14 (ESV)

One summer afternoon, the grandparents came into town, and we headed to our favorite restaurant, which sits beside heavily trafficked train tracks—a toddler's dream come true!

My two-year-old, Jake, could hardly eat lunch he was so excited. He watched from inside the restaurant as a few trains zipped by, then practically leaped from his seat when it was time to go sit on the platform and watch them up close. The trains that come through don't stop here. They zip through at a somewhat alarming rate, even from our safe spot on the platform.

Jake wasn't prepared for the noise the engines made or the shrill shriek of the whistle as the kindhearted engineer tooted the horn.

He turned to his sister, Olivia, who had covered her ears. She jumped up and ran to him, putting her hands over his ears instead. Of course, her ears were now bare. Olivia had been here before and liked her ears covered when the trains passed, but it was Jake's first time. She looked back at us, pained by the noise, until Poppa put his hands over her ears. Olivia motioned to her grandma, KK, to put her hands over Poppa's ears.

Brian and I laughed at the little ear-covering train we had going on there on the train's platform—all because Olivia was willing to put Jake's comfort above her own.

There are people who stand frozen from inexperience or fear and those who leap to action, doing what they can to help others. I'm thankful for Olivia's willing spirit and God-given empathy and her willingness to share those gifts with her little brother.

Let Us Pray

Lord, help me raise good-hearted, kind children who are tuned in to the needs of those around them. It would be my honor and my life's greatest work.

Further Reflection

PSALM 103:13 (ESV)

As a father shows compassion to his children, so the LORD shows compassion to those who fear him.

LAMENTATIONS 3:32 (ESV)

But, though he cause grief, he will have compassion according to the abundance of his steadfast love.

COLOSSIANS 3:12 (ESV)

Put on then, as God's chosen ones, holy and beloved, compassionate hearts, kindness, humility, meekness, and patience.

Awesomeville

VICKI KUYPER

You have turned my mourning into dancing; you took off my sackcloth and clothed me with a garment of joy.

PSALM 30:11 (ISV)

It was a sign from God. Not a burning bush, a rainbow, or a plague of frogs, but a wooden sign tucked in the corner of a folksy gift shop in Bluffton, South Carolina. Bold white letters on a black background proclaimed this: *Welcome to Awesomeville! Population: Me.*

Yep. The sign stopped me in my tracks. After thirty-three years of marriage, my husband had left—suddenly, unexpectedly, and permanently. Newly single, I felt like an awkward adolescent, unsure of what to do with my life. But I wasn't sixteen. I was almost sixty. And I had a choice. I could choose bitterness, anger, and fear as my new companions. Or I could embrace forgiveness, hope, and joy. I could choose to exist in Woe-Is-Me Town or thrive in Awesomeville. I knew where I wanted to reside.

I brought my sign from God home to my new little apartment. It still hangs right by my front door. It's a daily reminder that my circumstances don't have the final say in what my life looks like. My attitude, choices, and faith (or lack thereof) set the tone each day.

That doesn't mean my residence in Awesomeville is painless. Plenty of days my heart still aches, and tears seem to come out of nowhere. But I don't have to live in a permanent state of bliss to continue to love life. Life can be hard, but nurturing a relationship with God doesn't have to be. I may be by myself, but as God reminds me daily, I'm never alone.

Let Us Pray

Dear Lord, open my eyes to the beauty and blessing of each new day, even the tough ones. Draw near to me in a way that makes Your presence more tangible in my life.

Further Reflection

JAMES 1:1–4 (ISV)

From: James, a servant of God and of the Lord Jesus, the Messiah. To: The twelve tribes in the Dispersion. Greetings. Consider it pure joy, my brothers, when you are involved in various trials, because you know that the testing of your faith produces endurance. But you must let endurance have its full effect, so that you may be mature and complete, lacking nothing.

Embracing Change

PATTY KIRK

*The one sitting on the throne said,
"See, I am making all things new!"*

REVELATION 21:5 (ISV)

The stream under the low-water bridge on my run used to
be full of crawdads. Now it's full of small white-and-silver
sardine-looking fish. They spend the day leaping relentlessly
straight up from the water and then splashing back down.

I'm afraid to research them—or what seems to be the
apparent emigration, or demise, of the crawfish. I'm certain
the Internet will confirm my fears. Earth is warming, melting,
changing. It seems the end of the ecosystem as I know it is happening all around me.

I don't know why these changes seem so ominous. In other
scenarios, I welcome change. I love when one season morphs
into the next, when the sunlit sky curdles into needed or even
unneeded rain. Rain—all precipitation, fog, snow, ice—is always wonderful, so full of nourishment and freshness and relief,
but I love when it stops, too, and the hot sun returns.

Seasonal changes are cyclical, though. I know the rain or
sun will come again. The crawdads' disappearance might not be
cyclical. Nonrecurrent change, even change for the good, means

loss. I loved when my magnificent infant daughters became women I could talk to, but in the process, I lost their tiny, perfect baby selves.

Losing what is beloved or familiar means entering the unknown, and that's alarming. Part of me shudders when I read John's prophecy of "new heaven and a new earth, because the first heaven and the first earth had disappeared, and the sea was gone" (Revelation 21:1, ISV). I love this earth and ocean, these crawdads, my daughters. I don't want any of them to be no more.

But in the new heaven and earth, John goes on to reveal, "There won't be death anymore. There won't be any grief, crying, or pain" (Revelation 21:4, ISV). I can look forward to losses like that!

Let Us Pray

Lord Jesus, help me welcome change instead of fearing it.

Further Reflection

JOHN 14:2 (ISV)

There are many rooms in my Father's house. If there weren't, I wouldn't have told you that I am going away to prepare a place for you, would I?

REVELATION 21:3–4 (ISV)

I heard a loud voice from the throne say, "See, the tent of God is among humans! He will make his home with them, and they will be his people. God himself will be with them, and he will be their God. He will wipe every tear from their eyes. There won't be death anymore. There won't be any grief, crying, or pain, because the first things have disappeared."

Love in the Face of Fear

DANIEL SCHANTZ

There is no fear in love.

1 JOHN 4:18 (KJV)

Don't forget," Sharon said to me at breakfast, "we are going to the open house today for that new business in town. There will be lots of important people there."

My stomach tightened. Meeting new people is hard for an introvert like me.

On the way to the open house, I watched a small plane land at our airport, and my mind drifted back to my childhood. I grew up in the village of New Antioch, Ohio, just south of the Wright-Patterson Air Force Base. A steady flow of aircraft flew low over our house every day, and for some reason it frightened me. The big transport planes sounded mournful, crawling across the sky, and the jets arrived with a boom that startled me.

My father must have sensed my fear, because one day he pointed to a transport plane and said, "That's a Gooney Bird, a DC-3. One of the best planes ever built." The next day, he brought me a picture book of airplanes, and I tried to identify the planes that flew overhead. The more interested I got in airplanes, the less I was afraid of them.

"Here we are," Sharon said, pointing to the entrance of the open house.

Drawing on my memory, I approached the strangers with interest instead of anxiety, probing them with questions: "Are you folks new to Missouri?" "Are your children getting adjusted to school?" "Exactly what do you do here?"

Turns out, I had a good time and actually made some new friends.

I am learning that it's hard to be interested in people and afraid of them at the same time.

Let Us Pray

Lord, You made me shy, but You gave me a good heart. Help me always to listen to my heart.

Further Reflection

ISAIAH 58:10 (KJV)

And if thou draw out thy soul to the hungry, and satisfy the afflicted soul; then shall thy light rise in obscurity, and thy darkness be as the noon day.

LUKE 2:46 (KJV)

And it came to pass, that after three days they found him in the temple, sitting in the midst of the doctors, both hearing them, and asking them questions.

Trusting a Horse— and God

ERIKA BENTSEN

Whenever I am afraid, I will trust in You.

PSALM 56:3 (NKJV)

Trust. That was what God had been teaching me.

I searched the tack room, but I couldn't find Jack's bridle anywhere. After four years, I'd forgotten which one was his. Someone at the ranch had been using his bridle on another horse, but which one? Nobody I could ask was around.

I'd never gone more than a month without riding, until I'd suffered career-ending back injuries. I was hurt while fighting a wildfire on the ranch where I'd lived for twenty years. Trust God through that? It took four painful years after the first surgery failed before my lesson climaxed and I underwent spine reconstruction. Six months and one day after that successful surgery, my doctor gave me approval to ride—but here I was, without a bridle.

I walked to the horses grazing on the hillside. Jack thrust his nose against me. "We have to wait a little longer," I said, rubbing his forehead. I must trust God in this delay too.

Jack snorted. My hand trailed along his neck as he started to move off. Then he stopped below me, my hand on the crest of his shoulder, his back waist-high. He waited. It wasn't planned. My leg swung up, and I was on. For a moment, the pain, the heartache, and the uncertainty of the past four years was gone. It was just me and Jack.

He tensed. I stiffened. Had I made a mistake? Should I have waited? Would he buck? Trust. I let go of fear. We both relaxed. Jack trotted to the other horses and dropped his head to graze. God was and is in control. I could look confidently at the world once again and know that through His grace I am healed.

Let Us Pray

Praise You for making me rely on You—not on myself.
I trust You, especially when I cannot see the way ahead.
I am safe in the shadow of Your wings.

Further Reflection

PSALM 73:28 (NKJV)

But it is good for me to draw near to God; I have put my trust in the Lord GOD, that I may declare all Your works.

PROVERBS 3:5 (NKJV)

Trust in the LORD with all your heart, and lean not on your own understanding.

Walking with God

AMY EDDINGS

*He Himself . . . might free those
who through fear of death were subject
to slavery all their lives.*

HEBREWS 2:14–15 (NASB1995)

As I walked down the sidewalk to church, I spotted a squirrel lying in the grass of someone's front lawn. I knew something was wrong, for I was almost upon him before he tried to move toward the safety of a nearby hickory tree.

I stopped to watch him. Was he injured? Could I help? He stood in the lawn, wavering on his little brown legs. He closed his eyes. His body sagged a little toward the grass. Then, smelling my nearness, he opened his eyes and tried again to run to the tree. Instead, he carved a wobbly circle in the grass, his head tilted to one side as if the weight were too much to bear.

He's dying, I thought. *Maybe he's been poisoned.*

"It's OK, little guy," I whispered, stretching out my hand in a parting blessing. "Lay it down."

The image stayed with me all day. At night, as I lay back against the pillows, I was seized with fear of dying. *Will it hurt?* I thought. *Was that squirrel in pain? Did he know he was dying? Was he fighting it? Will I?* My heart raced. My breathing grew shallow and my chest tight. I was having a panic attack. I couldn't go to sleep. It felt too much like dying.

I prayed for the feeling to pass. I prayed that great comforting psalm: Psalm 23. My heart slowed. My soul quieted down.

I do not know if death will hurt. I do not know if I will fight, like the squirrel, or lay my soul down readily. But in faith, I believe God will not let me walk that journey alone. Trusting in that belief, I'll find freedom from the fear of death.

Let Us Pray

**God, death is not my enemy—fear of death is.
Give me courage in my hour of need!**

Further Reflection

PSALM 23:4 (NASB)

Even though I walk through the valley of the shadow of death, I fear no evil, for You are with me; Your rod and Your staff, they comfort me.

PSALM 31:5 (NASB)

Into Your hand I entrust my spirit; You have redeemed me, LORD, God of truth.

1 CORINTHIANS 15:22, 51 (NASB)

For as in Adam all die, so also in Christ all will be made alive. . . . Behold, I am telling you a mystery; we will not all sleep, but we will all be changed.

Not So Different after All

PAM KIDD

Thy kingdom come.

MATTHEW 6:10 (KJV)

In a poor village in Appalachia, where David and I began our marriage while serving as missionaries, we were shocked to learn that our little Presbyterian congregation had a fear of Catholics. I wondered, *How do you reeducate those taught by a trusted minister to fear people who are different from themselves?*

David realized the congregation needed to meet some Catholic people to readjust their views, so he reached out. He invited Catholics, who were serving at a mission site on the other side of the mountain, to a joint ice cream social. The ice cream was churned, the tables were set, and the Catholics arrived.

Not one soul from our congregation came.

Soon after, some women in our congregation were chatting about how they had always wanted to learn to knit.

One phone call later, I had signed up a plainclothes nun to teach a knitting class. The church ladies gathered, amid yarn and needles, and fell in love with the kindly woman they fondly called "Teacher." I waited as we progressed to shawls and sweaters for the reveal.

"Did I ever tell you . . . Teacher is a nun from the mission?" Silence.

Then, "Teacher, can you show me that last stitch again?"

And there, at that mission site, a small group of Appalachian women, as Presbyterians and Catholics, bonded in mutual love.

There You are, God.

Let Us Pray

Father, Your kingdom keeps coming in unexpected ways. I am humbled to find You in the midst of it all.

Further Reflection

MATTHEW 6:10–13 (KJV)

Thy kingdom come, Thy will be done in earth, as it is in heaven. Give us this day our daily bread. And forgive us our debts, as we forgive our debtors. And lead us not into temptation, but deliver us from evil: For thine is the kingdom, and the power, and the glory, for ever. Amen.

Facing Ghosts

VICKI KUYPER

*I will take refuge in the shadow of your
wings until the disaster has passed.*

PSALM 57:1 (NIV)

Cue the *Ghostbusters* theme. My granddaughter tosses a
white, fuzzy blanket over her head and runs helter-skelter
around the kitchen, making eerie-sounding moans and groans.
"I ain't afraid of no ghosts!" she shouts. Then, sliding the blanket onto the floor, she adds quietly, "Except sometimes . . ."

I appreciate her honesty. I certainly know the feeling.
Although a fear of the supernatural doesn't rank high on my
list, plenty of other things go bump in the night, or at least
bump around in my overactive imagination, to set my heart
racing and make me want to hide under the covers. I think
that's why I watch police procedurals and a few semi-creepy
television shows. I want what I fear to be contained, explained,
and have everything come out OK in the end. Preferably in
under an hour.

However, watching reruns of *Sherlock* or *The X-Files* isn't
the most effective strategy when fear creeps into my life. In
Psalm 56:3 (NIV), David captures God's solution rather simply:
"When I am afraid, I put my trust in you." Figuring out how to
trust God in concrete, practical ways isn't always that simple. It
doesn't mean I turn a blind eye to my fears and hum "Amazing

Grace." It means I face my fears, head-on, trusting that God is by my side.

In truth, most of my deepest fears stem from my own insecurities. They creep in from the inside. That's when I need to take refuge in the shadow of God's wings through honest prayer. It's like hiding under a blanket that provides the courage I need to face what I fear most.

Let Us Pray

**Dear Lord, You're my sword and shield,
my refuge and strength. Help me trust in
You more than in my own abilities.**

Further Reflection

PSALM 34:4 (NIV)

I sought the LORD, and he answered me; he delivered me from all my fears.

PSALM 118:6–7 (NIV)

The LORD is with me; I will not be afraid. What can mere mortals do to me? The LORD is with me; he is my helper. I look in triumph on my enemies.

Look for Signs

MARILYN TURK

*Cast all your anxiety on him
because he cares for you.*

1 PETER 5:7 (NIV)

I watched my husband, Chuck, walk away from us at the Sydney Airport, my stomach in knots. *Lord, please help me do this.*

We'd traveled to Australia to celebrate Christmas with Chuck's son, his wife, and their two boys. Logan, the seven-year-old grandson who lived with us, accompanied us on the trip. But he had to return to school soon afterward, so I agreed to take him back home by myself. Chuck wanted to stay longer and spend more time with his family he hadn't seen for two and a half years since they moved.

We'd never been to Australia before, and Chuck handled all the arrangements in our multileg journey, navigating our way there. Now I was traveling back without him, and I was worried about the trip because I had to look out for Logan as well as find our way through several busy airports. Fear of getting separated from the child had my nerves on edge.

Logan pulled on my hand, and I peered down at his inquisitive face. "Where are we going now, Grandma?"

Not wanting to show him my anxiety, I told him to search for the number of our gate. I pointed to the various signs posted overhead. "It's on one of the signs that says, 'Departures.'"

"There it is!" Logan pointed to a screen to our left.

Sure enough, he'd found the correct one. I was amazed at how much his reading skill had advanced in second grade. From that moment on, I asked him to help me find every sign we needed to navigate through the airports, and he did quite well. He even insisted on pulling the heaviest suitcases to show how grown up he'd become.

Halfway home, I realized I was no longer nervous about our trip and that I didn't have to look out for Logan. He was looking out for me.

Let Us Pray

Lord, help me remember that I don't need to worry since our lives are in Your hands.

Further Reflection

LUKE 12:25–26 (NIV)

Who of you by worrying can add a single hour to your life? Since you cannot do this very little thing, why do you worry about the rest?

Freed from Fear

KIM TAYLOR HENRY

There is a time for everything, and a season for every activity under the heavens.

ECCLESIASTES 3:1 (NIV)

I've never been much of a bucket-list person. If ever something was on mine, it was to visit Jerusalem and the Holy Land. But for years, fear of danger had kept me away. Then a tour invitation popped up on social media and something inside me said, "Go!" We booked the trip.

I've read the Bible through many times, but I never paid much attention to where those divine events took place. Locations were simply names attached to vague, conjured images of quaint, dusty villages, a manger scene, or camel-hued earth. Then, amazingly, I was there, standing, walking, gazing on holy ground. I saw Nazareth, Jerusalem, Cana, the Sea of Galilee, the Mount of Olives, Gethsemane, the Jordan River, the Valley of Armageddon, and Mount Zion. I visited the places where Jesus multiplied the loaves and fishes, where Elijah challenged Baal worshippers to a fire contest, and where Jesus was

baptized. My head spun. Locations were no longer words to be skimmed over. The Bible was coming to life in a new way.

To say that I was overwhelmed is an understatement. There was more than I could absorb, most of it quite different from what I'd expected. But what surprised me most was the absence of fear. From the moment I booked the reservations, through nine days of assimilating all I saw, not once was I afraid. God filled me with peace as he showed me his beloved land.

Let Us Pray

Thank You, Lord, for taking away my fear and telling me it was time to experience Your sacred land.

Further Reflection

ISAIAH 41:10 (NIV)

So do not fear, for I am with you; do not be dismayed, for I am your God. I will strengthen you and help you; I will uphold you with my righteous right hand.

ISAIAH 54:14 (NIV)

In righteousness you will be established: Tyranny will be far from you; you will have nothing to fear. Terror will be far removed; it will not come near you.

From Doubts to Done

CAROL KUYKENDALL

When I am afraid, I put my trust in you.
In God, whose word I praise—in God
I trust and am not afraid.

PSALM 56:3–4 (NIV)

I wake up scared some nights with a painful gnawing in my
stomach. Then I remember. I'm facing a seemingly impossible
writing deadline that feels too big and too complicated. Instead
of making progress, I'm getting increasingly tangled in the process. In the darkness, my fears start growing beyond the writing
project. What if my brain can't handle hard challenges? What if
I don't have what it takes? What if I can't meet this deadline?

I wrote these words in my journal several months ago.
Rereading them now, I'm surprised by the depth of my doubts.
The writing project—a book manuscript—was one of the hardest things I've ever tackled, but it is finished. Now, I want to
remember how I got from *doubts* to *done*.

I told a friend about this, and she reminded me of Joshua
and the stone memorial. God told Joshua to lead the Israelites
across the Jordan River into the land He wanted to give them.
As they camped on the shore of the rushing, flood-stage waters, they must have tried to fall asleep, fearing the seemingly
impossible task ahead of them. Were they capable? Did they
trust God to provide what they needed? The next morning as

they stepped into the water, the river stopped flowing and they crossed over on dry ground. God then told them to take stones from the river and build a memorial to remind them that He provides what is needed when it is needed.

Joshua's story reminds me that God didn't give me what I needed in the middle of the night but in the morning when I sat down to write. Page by page, I met my deadline. Now, the finished book will be my stone memorial, a reminder of God's power and faithfulness.

Let Us Pray

Lord, help us trust Your faithfulness, even in the dark.

Further Reflection

JOSHUA 3:4 (NIV)

Then you will know which way to go, since you have never been this way before. But keep a distance of about two thousand cubits between you and the ark; do not go near it.

2 CORINTHIANS 12:9 (NIV)

But he said to me, "My grace is sufficient for you, for my power is made perfect in weakness." Therefore I will boast all the more gladly about my weaknesses, so that Christ's power may rest on me.

PHILIPPIANS 1:6 (NIV)

. . . being confident of this, that he who began a good work in you will carry it on to completion until the day of Christ Jesus.

Someone Is Looking Out for You

ERIKA BENTSEN

*In Your hand is power and might; in
Your hand it is to make great and
to give strength to all.*

1 CHRONICLES 29:12 (NKJV)

My husband, Randy, calls at nine in the morning. "A lineman has been burned on the 500-kV transmission line. I don't know how badly. He needs prayers. They're flying him to the burn center in Portland."

Calls like this are a kick in the gut, another opportunity for fear to whisper: *This could be Randy.* My husband is a lineman with the power company. I pray fervently for his safety every day. My hands shake as I type a message to my battalion of prayer warriors.

Electrical burns are devastating. Extremities are most vulnerable. They can even affect one's personality permanently.

Lord, be merciful. Envelop them in Your love. Give them hope and healing. It's not just the linemen I pray for; it's their wives and children. It takes a special kind of person to be a line worker. Risking their lives is their everyday job. It isn't easy being a lineman's wife either. Coping with the danger affects the whole family. All we can do for our loved ones is pray they make it home each day. Often, that doesn't feel like enough.

Two somber days pass. Randy calls again in midmorning. This time he's ecstatic. "Your prayers worked! The lineman has been released. He has feeling in both hands and can use his legs. The burn center can't explain it. He took a direct hit and fell a long way, but his injuries are minor. The second man wasn't hurt at all. They said Someone was looking out for them."

I hang up and text my prayer warriors, praising God. That same Someone is looking out for my Randy too.

Let Us Pray

Please, Lord, bless the line workers who risk their lives every day. Keep their hands steady and bring them home safely. Comfort their families; You are protecting their loved ones on the line.

Further Reflection

DEUTERONOMY 31:6 (NKJV)

Be strong and of good courage, do not fear nor be afraid of them; for the LORD your God, He is the One who goes with you. He will not leave you nor forsake you.

PSALM 86:5 (NKJV)

For You, Lord, are good, and ready to forgive, and abundant in mercy to all those who call upon You.

PHILIPPIANS 4:7 (NKJV)

. . . and the peace of God, which surpasses all understanding, will guard your hearts and minds through Christ Jesus.

Branches and Vines

DANIEL SCHANTZ

*As the branch cannot bear fruit of itself,
unless it abides in the vine, neither can
you, unless you abide in Me.*

JOHN 15:4 (NKJV)

On Tuesday, Jesus—who was always teaching—told his disciples a parable about some vinedressers. The "vine" was a favorite analogy of his, and some of his most serious admonitions were about vines: "I am the vine, you are the branches. . . . without Me you can do nothing" (John 15:5, NKJV).

I thought of this passage recently, when I was preparing a commencement speech. The harder I worked on it, the more frustrated I became.

One night, I had a flashback to one of my first days in the classroom as a college professor, when I went to class unprepared. I had worked hard on the lesson but had only enough material for about ten minutes. I shuffled into class, resigned to failure.

Five minutes into the lecture, a student asked a question. While I pondered it, another student answered his fellow classmate. Soon the whole class was crackling with discussion on the topic I had introduced. I just tweaked the discussion, and it turned out to be one of the best classes of the semester. It was good for me to learn, early on, that teaching is not all up to me. It's a partnership with God and students.

The next day, I looked at my commencement notes and realized that I was overpreparing. I had not allowed any room for the Spirit to work. I put the notes away. On the night of commencement, I dusted them off, talked to God about my fears and hopes, and then delivered a speech that was "ours," not "mine."

When facing such frustrations, I need to remember that I am just a branch. God is the vine, my secret source of nourishment.

Let Us Pray

Thank You, Father, for the peace of mind that comes from realizing that success is not all up to me.

Further Reflection

PROVERBS 11:28 (NKJV)

He who trusts in his riches will fall, but the righteous will flourish like foliage.

PROVERBS 28:26 (NKJV)

He who trusts in his own heart is a fool, but whoever walks wisely will be delivered.

Calm the Storms of Your Life

LOGAN ELIASEN

Blessed is the one who trusts in the LORD, whose confidence is in him.

JEREMIAH 17:7 (NIV)

The store employee squinted as she surveyed the wall of laptop chargers. I drummed my fingers on my jeans. The final paper for my labor law class was due tomorrow, and I hadn't anticipated replacing a fried computer charger. I had already wasted an hour.

That's when the storm sirens started—loud and mournful. They were accompanied by an announcement over the loudspeaker.

"Attention, customers. A tornado warning has been issued. The store is now closed. Please seek shelter in the back of the store."

"You're kidding me," I said. The employee shook her head.

I followed a line of customers to a break room. The sirens continued their death knell to any plans of finishing my paper.

As I sat with the crowd of people, I couldn't stop thinking about the paper. My heart beat faster, seeming to match the pace of the rain on the roof. The woman next to me stared at her phone. The weather radar on her screen blipped as she twisted and untwisted a lock of hair. She was also nervous, but her fear was focused on the weather.

The weather didn't bother me. I trusted that I'd come out safely.

Why could I be so sure of God's power over a tornado but unwilling to trust that He would help me complete a paper? I was comfortable relinquishing my physical safety to God, but not my GPA. But the God who calmed storms also cared about the intimate details of my life. I needed to learn to entrust those details to Him.

"Good news," the store manager said. "The tornado is passing, and the store will be reopening soon."

Finally, I was glad to be free to leave. But there was even greater freedom in remembering to trust God.

Let Us Pray

Lord, help me to entrust all areas of my life to You.

Further Reflection

PSALM 143:8 (NIV)

Let the morning bring me word of your unfailing love, for I have put my trust in you. Show me the way I should go, for to you I entrust my life.

PROVERBS 3:5–6 (NIV)

Trust in the LORD with all your heart and lean not on your own understanding; in all your ways submit to him, and he will make your paths straight.

I See You

JULIA ATTAWAY

Through you we push back our enemies;
through your name we trample our foes.

PSALM 44:5 (NIV)

I didn't want to make the phone call. The last time I'd spoken with our landlord things had not gone well. Despite the time sensitivity of what I needed to discuss, I avoided dialing the number.

All morning, I reminded myself to make the call. All morning, I didn't do it.

What's going on? I finally asked myself after lunch. *Why are you avoiding this? You've made plenty of uncomfortable calls in your life.*

The answer came promptly: *I'm afraid.*

Startled by what should have been obvious, I was astonished at how adroitly fear had wafted into my heart. But giving my amorphous discomfort a name made it easier to address.

"I see you, Fear," I said to his wispy face, "and now that I do, I need you to step aside." Caught, he floated off a bit, sulking at being called out. I took a deep breath. I took another.

Then I dialed my landlord's number, still mildly uncomfortable but thinking more clearly. I was not unhappy that the call went to voicemail. I left a message.

By the time I hung up, Fear had vanished.

Let Us Pray

Lord, help me to see and name my fears so that
I can push them back in Your name.

Further Reflection

JOSHUA 1:9 (NIV)

Have I not commanded you? Be strong and courageous.
Do not be afraid; do not be discouraged, for the LORD
your God will be with you wherever you go.

PSALM 118:6 (NIV)

The LORD is with me; I will not be afraid. What can mere
mortals do to me?

JOHN 14:27 (NIV)

Peace I leave with you; my peace I give you. I do not give
to you as the world gives. Do not let your hearts be troubled and do not be afraid.

"Come to Me"

DESIREE COLE

See! I stand at the door and knock.
If anyone hears my voice and opens
the door, I will come in to him.

REVELATION 3:20 (CSB)

Things weren't going according to plan. It had been four
months since my husband, Zach, and I left New York City
to move back to my hometown in Kansas. I thought by now I'd
have a job. Maybe a new house. But there'd been one roadblock
after another.

Instead of locking eyes with Jesus, I was getting distracted
by fear. It was getting harder to hear His voice as time went on.

One morning at church, our pastor called a small prayer
team to the front. The lights dimmed, leaving the room bathed
in only candlelight. The worship band's melody saturated the
room with God's Spirit. Then, a whisper in the air dug its
way down into my heart. God wanted me to go forward to
be prayed for. But I resisted moving. I was afraid that I didn't
know what to ask the team members to pray for me.

When I got up there, no one on the prayer team was available. Others had followed their nudges before I did. So I stood
there, alone. Humiliated! People in the front rows stared at me.

I was about to go back to my seat when something caught
my attention. A middle-aged man on the prayer team had

emerged from a dark corner of the room. He walked toward me, smiling, motioning to come to him. The scene gripped my heart.

I realized that Jesus does this for me every day, especially when I feel lost or misplaced. He walks toward me, waving me closer. His attention is only on me. "Come to Me," I hear from Him. "I'll talk to Father about what you need."

Let Us Pray

Jesus, You always find a way to catch my eye at just the right time and offer to do what I can't.

Further Reflection

ZEPHANIAH 3:17 (CSB)

The LORD your God is among you, a warrior who saves. He will rejoice over you with gladness. He will be quiet in his love. He will delight in you with singing.

ROMANS 8:38–39 (CSB)

For I am persuaded that neither death nor life, nor angels nor rulers, nor things present nor things to come, nor powers, nor height nor depth, nor any other created thing will be able to separate us from the love of God that is in Christ Jesus our Lord.

Author Index

A Note from the Editors

We hope you enjoyed *Faith over Fear*, published by Guideposts. For over 75 years, Guideposts, a nonprofit organization, has been driven by a vision of a world filled with hope. We aspire to be the voice of a trusted friend, a friend who makes you feel more hopeful and connected.

By making a purchase from Guideposts, you join our community in touching millions of lives, inspiring them to believe that all things are possible through faith, hope, and prayer. Your continued support allows us to provide uplifting resources to those in need. Whether through our communities, websites, apps, or publications, we inspire our audiences, bring them together, and comfort, uplift, entertain, and guide them. Visit us at guideposts.org to learn more.

We would love to hear from you. Write us at Guideposts, P.O. Box 5815, Harlan, Iowa 51593, or call us at (800) 932-2145. Did you love *Faith over Fear*? Leave a review for this product on guideposts.org/shop. Your feedback helps others in our community find relevant products.

Find inspiration, find faith, find Guideposts.
Shop our best sellers and favorites at
guideposts.org/shop
Or scan the QR code to go directly to our Shop